T0367504

As Far As You Know

AS FAR AS YOU KNOW

Carolann Plank

authorHOUSE®

AuthorHouse™
1663 Liberty Drive
Bloomington, IN 47403
www.authorhouse.com
Phone: 1-800-839-8640

© 2012 Carolann Plank. All rights reserved.

No part of this book may be reproduced, stored in
a retrieval system, or transmitted by any means
without the written permission of the author.

First published by AuthorHouse 3/21/2012

ISBN: 978-1-4685-5609-4 (e)
ISBN: 978-1-4685-5608-7 (sc)

Printed in the United States of America

Any people depicted in stock imagery provided by Thinkstock are
models, and such images are being used for illustrative purposes only.
Certain stock imagery © Thinkstock.

This book is printed on acid-free paper.

Because of the dynamic nature of the Internet, any web addresses or
links contained in this book may have changed since publication and
may no longer be valid. The views expressed in this work are solely
those of the author and do not necessarily reflect the views of the
publisher, and the publisher hereby disclaims any responsibility for them.

I dedicate my first book to my best friend, Amanda. She had faith in me from the beginning of this project, and without her support, I very well may have scrapped this story and forgotten all about it. I would also like to thank everyone who was involved in publishing my first book. Your help made my dream come true. I couldn't have made it this far without you. Lastly, I would like to thank Suzanne Collins for her wonderful trilogy of *The Hunger Games*, which inspired me instantly to write and create stories.

PART ONE

CHAPTER 1

I walk into a room; the air is filled with smog, and I cough. I get closer and closer to Elle until our hands almost touch, and she disappears. But before she can vanish out of sight, I hear a faint whimper. I squint into the darkness and slowly take one more step toward where my sister once was.

"Elle," I whisper. I hear the whimper again, and I run in that direction. I see her on the floor, sprawled out and crying. I cautiously step nearer and nearer to her. She looks up at me and struggles to stand up. "Elle!" I shriek, and she stops and smiles at me with a full head of razor-sharp teeth and then looks down. Our eyes stop at her hip, which is bloody, with her skin torn unevenly. She creeps toward me and leaps.

I wake with a jump, and Elle is on top of me, her eyes locked on mine. "Hey, Elle," I say, and she jumps off of me and lands on the floor next to my bed. "Just a bad dream," I assure her.

"Okay, but it's the fourth one this week!" she protests. "Why won't you tell me about them?" She knows why, but she loves to argue with me.

"They are too scary," I tell her again. She just rolls her eyes.

"You're eight. I'll tell you when you're older," I assure her.

She frowns and starts to pout. "But what if you forget them?" she asks.

I sit up and ruffle her short brown hair. "It'd be better if I did forget, and you never know!" I say and get out of bed. Elle follows me, staying on my heels until I reach my dresser.

"Please!" she begs.

"No!" I say, and she storms out of the room. I change out of my pajamas and slip on my brown shirt that has tears at the ends of the sleeves and a pair of my light blue jeans with a big hole in one knee. I brush my hair with the wooden brush that my aunt gave me three years ago and braid it down the back. I slip on my shoes and yell to Elle that I'm going to the woods.

"Wait for me!" she calls and comes out of her room, pulling on her shoes.

"Fine," I grunt, and she smiles huge, showing small white teeth. Nothing compared to what she looked like in the dream. I shiver, and Elle sees me.

"Your dream was about me, wasn't it?" she asks with a shallow voice.

"No. I mean, yes. I mean, I'll tell you later!" I stutter.

Looking at her expression, she doesn't seem satisfied with my response, but she doesn't say anything. I hold the door open for her, and she walks out. Her hair blows in the wind, and I close the wooden door with a slam and step outside as well. The air is thick and moist, just like in that room in my dream. I try to shake the thought of it and catch up with Elle. She clings to my side as soon as I am next to her.

"I don't tell you my dreams because I'm trying to protect you as long as possible," I whisper to her softly. She stares straight ahead and stands on her toes, motioning me to lower myself to her level so she can whisper something. Her breath is warm as she speaks into my ear.

"I have nightmares too," she says. I look around because I have a strange feeling we are being watched. "I dream about you climbing walls and ceilings. You have a scary face; your eyes are all black, and so is your mouth."

I freeze in place and stare at her. Elle breaks apart from me and takes a step back. "How can you tell it's me?" I ask, but I really don't want to know.

"Because you always whisper, 'Elle, save me!' and then you smile with pointy teeth." That last part scares me, and I can tell that Elle knows it when she strokes my arm to comfort me.

A feeling of uneasiness comes over me. I'm not sure if it's what Elle said or if it's something else. "Stay here," I say and push her behind me. "I'll be right back." I walk deeper into the woods.

I pull out the knife that I carry in my boot and grip it tightly. Readying it in case anyone, or anything, tries to attack me. I use this knife to cut up game when I hunt. I pick up the pace and look around and stop suddenly when I see an object move. I tighten my grip around the handle of the knife. I strain to see if it's an animal. I move in closer trying not to make any noise. I see it move in between the trees and this time I know what it is.

I turn back to where Elle is standing. "Elle!" I scream.

"Don't move!" With that, I charge after it. I trample every branch, leaf, and twig that gets in my way. The person is running from me, but I can't tell if it's anyone I know. A thick coating of dirt is smothered all over his or her face, and his or her hair is just as dirty. I force myself to keep running faster and faster until I can hear the person panting. I reach my arm out to grab him or her and yank the person back onto the ground with me. I quickly get to my feet, as the other person is struggling to get up. I can tell it's a he now. I grab his collar and pull him towards me.

"Why were you spying on me and my little sister?" I demand.

He raises his hands and shrugs his shoulders. "Why were you walking around at six in the morning?" he asks with a laugh.

But I can sense fear, and he is terrified. "I asked you first! Why were you snooping?" I yell.

He tugs at my hands and frees his shirt. "I was going swimming when I heard voices, so I went to go check it out. I saw you and who else?"

I huff. "My sister!" I say, annoyed. I don't bother to hide it either; the more scared of me he is, the better.

"Right, you and your sister. Anyway, I wanted to see where you guys were going to, and that is pretty much it."

I squint at him and push him back. I don't waste time flirting or playing nice with boys. I have better things to do with my precious time. He raises his eyebrows and looks at me like I've just lost my mind. "I'm sorry; I didn't introduce myself properly. Hi, my name is Ash Parker." He holds out his hand, but I'm already turning to leave.

"Serena," I say without turning back. Ash catches

up and stares at me. "Don't do that!" I say, backing away from him.

"What?" he asks, shocked.

"You were just staring at me!" I yell.

He is obviously playing stupid. "Yeah, so?" he asks.

I speed up and block the middle of the path with my body. "So, it's weird. I'm going back for Elle," I explain.

"Who?" he asks. I turn around and see that he has wiped almost all of the dirt off of his face.

"My sister, and since you like to talk so much, why don't you tell me why you're covered in dirt." He stops in his tracks, but I keep walking.

"I fell," he says. I stop and turn around to face him. I raise my eyebrows at him and turn my head to the side. "No really!" he insists. "I was climbing a hill to get to the lake over there, and I slid down." I don't even know why I bothered to ask. I turn on my heels and start sprinting towards Elle. I'm a fast runner and I doubt Ash can catch up to me.

"Serena!" I hear Elle call through the pine trees. "Serena!" she keeps on calling. Her voice sounds panicked. I try to run faster but there are so many branches and rocks blocking the path. I try to avoid anything that could cause me to trip and fall. I can't make out where she's at and when I think I'm close I run into Ash and falls down. I'm struggling to get around him, as he's struggling to get back up. I stop and hold out my hand to help him up.

"Elle! I'm coming!" I yell and start running again with Ash behind me. But before I can go far, Ash stops me. He grips my arm with his hand and refuses to let go. "Let me go!" I scream, and he covers my mouth with his hand.

"Shut up and listen!" he barks.

I stop squirming and listen. Elle's cries are bouncing off the trees. "She's in pain," he says and removes his hand from my face. I don't move for a few seconds trying to figure out in which direction to run. But I hear her cry in the distance and chase after the sound as fast as possible. On the edge of the field I see Elle. She lies curled up and crying. I rush over to her and ask her what's wrong. She can't talk, but I see two small holes on her ankle that look like a snake bite. "It looks like a snake bite," I murmur to myself.

Elle can't hear me; she's in her own world, staring into space, screaming. She's afraid of snakes and spiders. The snake scared her and she is traumatized from it biting her. Not even looking back, I can tell that Ash is not far behind me because of his heavy panting and the sound of the leaves crunching beneath his shoes.

"She got bit by a snake," I say, and he comes over.

He examines the marks and looks at me, puzzled. "I'm not sure if it was poisonous or not," I say.

He takes his hands and puts them on my right arm, and I flinch. "Relax," he says and yanks off my sleeve. He ties it around Elle's ankle right above the bite marks.

"The marks are a little lower than that," I tell him.

"I put it there so if it's poisonous, the venom will only eat away at that part of her ankle and not spread to the body," he explains as he tightens the torn sleeve. I watch him work.

"Why are you doing this?" I ask him.

He looks at me with a smile and says, "Because you need my help. Plus, I'm a nice guy. Haven't you figured that out yet?"

He sits on the ground next to Elle's feet and stares at her ankle as if he were trying to heal it with his thoughts. "We'll just wait about twenty minutes to see if the venom is poisonous, and if nothing happens to her ankle, we can remove the sleeve." I agree by nodding my head and staring at his face. I sit with Elle's head on my lap stroking her hair until she falls asleep. The twenty minutes pass by slowly, and nothing happens. We remove the clothing from her ankle and wait.

Elle eventually wakes up, and I tell her what happened. "You know I'm afraid of snakes. I didn't see it when I was sitting on the rock. My ankle still hurts." She nudges my arm when she sees Ash standing behind me. "Hey, who's he?" I look at Ash, and Elle smiles at him.

"Hey Ash, how old are you?" I call to him.

"Sixteen," he calls back.

Elle leans into me and whispers, "Ooh! You should totally go out with him!"

"I don't even know this guy!" I say and turn away from her.

"Oh, come on! He keeps staring at you, and he has a beautiful smile!" she points out.

I look over my shoulder and stare at him. Elle is right; he has a nice smile and kind eyes. He probably has a girlfriend, and if not, he could easily get a girlfriend if he wanted one. I continue to stare at his dirty blonde hair, mysterious brown eyes, and muscular body. *How could he have a hard time keeping up with me in the woods?* I don't care, but I am truly thankful that he saved Elle, and he is still being nice to me even though I was annoying earlier. If he asked me out, I wouldn't reject the offer.

"If you're feeling better we could go swimming, Elle.

How does that sound?" I say and poke her in the stomach. She giggles and agrees. "Hey Ash! Do you want to go swimming with us?" I ask him.

His face brightens up, and he sprints right over to us. "Sure!" he says and takes my hand. "I know a great river not far from here." With that, he leads Elle and me through the woods. After several minutes of walking, we stop next to a big tree, and Ash pushes the branches aside to let us go first. We walk through and see a beautiful river with sparkling clean water and little fish swimming through the water's shallow edge.

"Ash, it's amazing!" I say. He pulls his shirt off and kicks his boots off before plunging into the water. Elle jumps in after him. I take my boots off and place them by a tree. I run towards them and splash into the water. The water is warm at the top and cooler at the bottom. Elle splashes me in the face with the water, and I splash her back. Ash tries to join in, but Elle and I gang up on him and drench him. After about an hour, we get out and dry off in the sun.

"There's nothing like spending a Saturday with your friends, right?" Ash says.

"Right," Elle agrees.

"Oh shoot!" I say as I remember my plans for the afternoon.

"What?" Ash asks, his voice sounds concerned.

"Nothing real important," I tell him. "I was supposed to meet Liam in the town square at noon!" I get up quickly and apologize to Ash before I run off with Elle following close behind.

I barely see the square when Liam runs into me. "Ouch, Serena!" he jokes. "Why'd you do that?" I shove his shoulder, and he stops to look at me. "Serena, why are your clothes wet?"

I look at my clothes. From my braid to my feet, I'm still wet. "I just went swimming with Elle and…" I hesitate, turn away and in a low whisper, add, "and Ash. It's no big deal."

Liam looks away from me when I look at him, and I can tell he feels uncomfortable. "Oh, cool. I'm glad you had fun."

"Thanks," I say, but Liam sounded tense when he spoke. "Is everything okay?" I ask in my softest voice.

"Sure, sure, everything's fine," he growls and sees Elle and gives her a high five and a basket of raspberries. "I almost forgot," he says when we reach the square. "I'd like to give you these." He holds out two lemons in his hands. He pushes them toward me, and I take them.

"Thank you!" I say and give him a hug. "Here," I tell him and give him back a lemon. "We can each have one, and Elle will eat her raspberries." The three of us head home to eat our delicious treats, but Elle is halfway done with hers by the time we reach the house.

Liam, Elle, and I sit in the front yard and eat our snacks. Liam and I make faces when we bite into the lemon. We make sure to shut our eyes, so we don't get lemon juice in them. Elle wolfs down the berries in no time, but Liam and I just take our time and savor every bite. After our last bite, we toss the peels into the trash.

Elle stays behind while Liam and I go into the woods for a few hours for a walk. We enter the woods where Elle got bitten by the snake. I try to forget it, but Ash won't get out of my head. I don't try to compare Liam to Ash, but it's kind of hard not to. Ash's dirty blonde hair is thick and wavy, unlike Liam's straight black hair which isn't shiny or full or anything, really. And Ash's eyes are mysterious and dark, whereas Liam's blue eyes are focused and hard, but also kind. Liam has an amazing smile; it doesn't look fake, and he smiles when he wants to and doesn't when he doesn't feel like it. Liam doesn't force a smile, and Ash's smile looks sort of fake, like he doesn't know how to smile naturally. They are both tall and muscular. Liam's skin is a bit tanner than Ash's.

"Why didn't you go to school yesterday?" Liam's voice rings in my ears.

"Elle didn't feel well, so I stayed home and took care of her." She felt better this morning. Thoughts of my dream last night started creeping back into my mind.

"Well, you missed the big announcement that there's a dance coming up."

My eyes flicker to the ground. "Oh cool. Who did you ask?"

Liam fidgets with his fingers for a bit and looks at me. "No one, yet."

I can tell where he is going with this, but I only like him as a friend. "Liam, you're my best friend in the entire freaking world. But a dance? Together? That could ruin our friendship."

He looks down at his shoes and drags his feet on the ground, kicking leaves out of his way. "Who will you be going with?" he asks.

I can tell he wants me to answer with nobody, so I do.

"Then why can't you go with me to the dance?" he asks.

My hands untie my braid and let my brown hair down

which is still wet. "We are just friends, and you deserve someone better than me," I say and look straight ahead. My words had no effect on me, but they did have one on Liam.

"You know that I know what's right for me," he says and looks at me. "But if you don't trust me, just go with your new boyfriend Ash."

I stop and stomp my foot. "He is not my boyfriend!" I yell.

"But you'd rather go to the dance with him than me!" Liam starts to raise his voice.

"Who says I even want to go?" I shout back. I can tell that my last comment knocked Liam over the edge, and I start running deeper into the woods. I stop momentarily to feel around in my boot for my knife, but it's not there. I would never hurt Liam for any reason, but when he gets angry I feel a lot safer with my knife handy. I hear Liam running after me, and I run faster and further into the woods. I know that I can't outrun Liam, so I outsmart him. I dash through the trees, and he follows. I zigzag through the woods, but Liam keeps on my trail. I pick up a small rock and throw it behind me. It hits him and slows him down for a few seconds, but he continues on. I start to panic. There are no more rocks, and Liam is quickly gaining on me.

I dash for a tree and climb it. I don't stop until I'm on a thin branch that can barely hold me. Liam comes after me, but he doesn't make it up as far as I do and climbs back down. I hear him swear and kick the tree. He doesn't leave for an hour. That's the bad thing about him; whenever he gets mad, he doesn't know how to express his anger in nonviolent ways.

Several minutes pass and he comes back for me. He stretches his hand out. "Please come down, Serena." he says. But I stay in the tree until I'm sure that he has cooled down. "I'm sorry," he says again in a calm voice. I climb down and back away from him. "Serena, it won't happen again; I swear it!"

I just shake my head and run back home. I feel tears coming on, and I don't know why. Liam has gotten ticked so many times before, and I haven't cried. Maybe it's because he is right; maybe I won't accept the fact that he's right for me. I run into the house and slam the door shut. I lean my back on the door and fall to the ground. Tears start rolling down my cheeks and into my mouth, and it taste salty.

Elle comes out of her bedroom and tries to comfort me. She tries to coax me to sit on the couch, but I prefer the floor. I don't tell her about Liam's rage issue and instead tell her that the neighbor's dog just died. She seems to believe it and tells me it's nothing to get upset about. I tell her that she's right, and I stop crying. Just as I stop, there's a knock on the door. I get up and open it.

Liam is there with his head down in shame; I don't feel sorry for him. "Can I come in?" he asks in a quiet voice.

"No," I say as forcefully as I can without crying again. "I don't want Elle to see you like this!" I say and slam the door in his face.

He opens it and pulls me outside. "I don't care!" he yells. "I told you I was sorry. Why won't you forgive me?"

I start to turn around, but he stops me. "Serena Coleman! Listen to me!" he screams at me. I turn around and spit in his face. He wipes it off, and I run inside and lock the door. Liam's fists pound against the door.

"Serena, open the door now!" he screams.

I bang on the door as well. "Shut up, Liam!" I scream as I walk away.

I find Elle and tell her to go into her bedroom and not to come out no matter what she hears. She runs to her room and locks herself in there.

I go back outside, and Liam is standing there. Angry and frustrated, he grabs my shoulders. I just stand there. "Why are you doing this?" I ask him. I can't help it any longer. I burst into tears, and he finally figures out how much he hurt me.

"I guess you don't want to go with me then?" he asks.

I peel his hands off me and hope he hears every word. "I am not going to the dance with you; I am going with Ash, and I hope whomever you marry will be able to deal with your fits, because I sure don't want to be thrown around like a rag doll every day! I hope that you will learn to control your anger!" And I walk past him.

It takes a minute for it to sink into his head, but when it does, I run as fast as I can through the woods to find Ash's river. I'm amazed I found it so easily. In front of me I find Ash sitting on the ground tossing small stones into the river. I come up behind him and he looks back and sees me staring at him. Panting, I tell him I'm just passing through. He nods, and I continue running along the river.

I look back and see Liam approaching Ash. I can't hear what they're saying, but I can tell they're quarrelling. I run towards them and observe Liam striking Ash in the nose. I see Ash holding his nose upward trying to stop the bleeding. Liam comes toward me, I push pass him focused on reaching Ash.

"Ash, are you okay?" I ask him.

"Yeah, sure." he says and lets go of his nose but keeps it upward. I grab Ash's arm. "Ash, we've got to go!"

I put myself between Liam and Ash. "If you want him, you have to go through me!" Liam grabs me by my waist, and I kick and lash at him. He carries me and sets me down a few feet away from Ash. He walks back over to Ash. I get up and run past Liam just as he pulled his arm back to hit Ash again. I jump in front of Ash, and Liam hits me in the head. I feel a sharp pain and then I pass out.

I wake up and see that I'm not by the river any longer. The room is unfamiliar and as I try to focus I see Liam standing over me. I roll onto my stomach and block my head with my hands. "Go!" I demand.

"No, I'm so sorry! How many times do I have to say it?" Liam says.

"Why are you even here?" I ask him angrily as I roll onto my back.

"I'm taking care of you," he says.

"No, you're not!" I say and push him away from me.

"Oh, and by the way, the dance is in two days. They announced it late."

I feel my face burning red. I explode, "You're seriously bringing up that stupid dance again? That's what got me here in the first place!" I take in a deep breath. "Is Ash here? Let me talk to Ash," I say through clenched teeth.

"No, he's not here," he claims. At that moment, I hear a loud banging sound. I sit straight up staring at the door. There's a sudden silence followed by heavy footsteps. The bedroom door flies open and standing in the doorway is Ash, a bruise covers his right cheek.

"Liam," I growl a harsh warning for him to leave, knowing the bruise on Ash's face came from his fist. "Get out, Liam! Now!" I yell.

Liam sluggishly moves across the room and hesitates at the door. "Good going, you made me a liar!" Liam hisses into Ash's ear, continuing to walk out, but stopping right outside the open door.

"Hey, Ash," I say trying to control my frustration. "I'm really sorry about Liam," I start to explain, "this is kind of last minute, but there's a school dance coming up, and well, I need someone to go with and—"

"Wait," Ash says, "Liam said that you were going with him."

My eyes squint at Liam. "Well I'm not!" I try to maintain my anger. Ash reaches behind him without looking and slams the door in Liam's face.

"Okay. Do you want to go with me to the dance?" Ash asks.

"Uh, sure! That would be great!" I say as I play with the ends of my hair. Ash smiles and turns to leave the room, when he opens the door Liam stumbles into the room, I laugh at him.

"What's so funny?" he asks me.

"Ash and I are going to the dance together! What am I going to wear?"

Liam grunts. "Wear something nice."

I roll my eyes. "Duh I'll wear something nice!" I can't stop smiling. Now I know I'm not the right girl for Liam. And for the first time in a long time, I feel like a weight has been lifted from my shoulders.

"By the way, how did I get here?" I ask feeling stupid for not asking before now. "Is this your bedroom?"

"Good guess," Liam replies. "I carried you here when you passed out. Do you remember what happened?"

I try to stand on my feet, but I wobble and collapse. I try again, this time holding on to Liam for support. This helps some but not much. I get frustrated and just fall back onto the wood floor. "Yes, I remember your fist colliding with my head." I say as he tries to help me up.

I shrug him off and start to drag myself across the floor in hopes of escape. Ash reaches down to help me up. I look up and notice the bruise on his nose and the bruise on his cheek looks worse close up. I take his hand and he picks me up like I'm a feather and puts me back on Liam's bed.

"Sorry about him," I whisper and touch the bruise on Ash's cheek. "Liam gets like that when he's angry."

Ash looks confused for a second when I touch his face. "My nose? No big deal. The only thing I'm worried about is that I'll still have this thing on the day of the dance."

I don't laugh, even though I know he was trying to humor me. "That's good," I say flatly and curl up in a ball in the sheets.

Ash and Liam leave, and Elle comes in. She runs to me, her light brown hair swinging on her way over. I open my arms, and she crawls into bed and curls up next to me.

"Why are you here? But more importantly, how'd you get here?" I ask her.

She shrugs and replies, "Ash stopped by our house to tell me what happened," she pauses before adding, "he was really worried about you." She inhales deeply and forces a smile. "So, how are you feeling?"

I laugh; she's the only person I ever laugh with besides Liam. "I feel horrible! I might die!" I say and let my tongue hang out of my mouth and close my eyes and pretend to be dead.

Elle giggles. "Oh no!" she screams sarcastically. We don't bother to keep our voices down.

"While we were gone from school, they announced that there will be a school dance. Liam told me about it," I say and sit up.

Elle mimics my movements until she is sitting up next to me. "Who are you going with?" she asks.

I smile and lean in close to her ear and whisper back, "Ash."

Elle gets excited and starts squealing with joy. "Ash! No way! That is so amazing!" she shrieks.

I put a finger to her lips and tell her to keep it down. I realize we were speaking loud. "Yeah, I'm excited too." I say quietly and take my finger away.

"Sorry," Elle apologizes.

I tell her it's okay and lay back down. Elle stays sitting up and looks around. "Serena, Ash is watching us," she whispers under her breath so I can barely hear it. I look over to where Elle was staring, and I see Ash moving away from the door out of sight. I didn't realize he was still around, but was glad that he cared enough to stay.

"Yeah, he was," I whisper and motion for her to turn around. She does, and I start braiding her hair down her back. It doesn't take long, because her hair is thin and short.

Ash comes into the room about a minute later; he

walks quickly and takes Elle by the hand and leads her out of the room. He moves towards me swiftly and flawlessly, his blonde hair falling into his eyes. I set my head on the pillow and close my eyes. I try to clear my mind but begin to picture Elle as she looked in my nightmare—fangs, scary, and controlled by something other than herself. I open my eyes, and Ash is sitting on the bed next to me. He is staring at me like he was in the woods.

"Don't do that!" I say with a half-hearted smile.

"What?" he asks, obviously not aware he was making me uncomfortable.

"You were staring at me!" I shriek.

He turns away for a second. "Sorry, I didn't know it bothered you," he laughs. I don't feel comfortable enough to laugh around him, so I snicker and push him over with my hands. He falls onto the wood floor with a thump, but he doesn't seem hurt. I guess if he can recover from a hit from Liam so quickly, he must be tough.

"Why didn't you hit Liam back?" I ask him when he picks himself off the floor.

"What do you mean?" he asks me.

"When he hit you, why didn't you hit back?" I ask again.

Ash takes a deep breath and sighs. "I didn't hit him because he is your friend, and I didn't want you to hate me for it."

I raise my eyebrows and my mouth drops open. "You didn't defend yourself because you thought I might hate you? I would hate you if you didn't hit him back; he needs to learn that hurting people isn't the answer." I feel out of breath by the time I finish explaining this to him.

Ash lowers his head. "So you hate me?" he asks and looks up with a puppy dog face.

It doesn't work on me, no matter who does it. I think if someone tries a puppy dog face on me, they are weak and don't know how to say what they think. "No, but if you were beating up Liam after he stopped fighting, I would personally rip your head off!" I say, and he backs away from me with a scared face. "He's my best friend. The only one I've ever really had other than my sister, Elle." I stare at the ceiling and notice the white paint fading into a dirty tan color.

"So you're a loner?" Ash teases me.

"Yep, Serena the loner," I tease back.

Liam walks into the room looking depressed. His features are worn and defenseless. It fools so many people, but I know better. Under that sappy surface is a hard, determined soul ready to do whatever it takes to get what it wants. I pull the blanket up to my chin and hope he won't notice me. I don't know what good it did me anyway.

"Elle and I were in the kitchen when we heard a noise," he says. His lips are cracked and pale pink.

"What kind of noise?" Ash asks him.

"Sort of like a gunshot," Liam replies with a hard face.

Ash rushes downstairs. I can barely make out what he's saying, but I can tell that he is asking Elle questions.

"Liam," I whisper. He turns to look at me. "I'm sorry," I say. Liam turns from me and walks out of the room.

I don't blame him for being mad at me. I would be mad at me too. I try to get up, this time with success. I'm a little shaky, so I walk carefully to the door and down the stairs.

I enter the kitchen, and Elle, Liam, and Ash turn their attention to me. I can tell by their faces that they are shocked that I made it downstairs without any help. My head starts to hurt again and my vision is getting blurry. I try to focus on Elle, but it's no use because now I'm seeing stars. I shake my head back and forth, trying to shake them away. This only makes it worse; my legs give out and I collapse to the floor. My hearing is fading as well. I can hear voices, but the sounds are muffled. All I can think about is how messed up I am, thanks to Liam's powerful punch!

Before I lose my hearing, I can hear Liam's voice. I can't make out what he is saying, so I just nod. I haven't lost feeling, though, so I feel someone pick me up and put me on a soft surface (most likely a couch). I feel around it with my fingers, stretching them as far as possible until they reach a small pillow. Yep, it's a couch. I reach out my hand, not knowing where. But when a pair of small fingers touches my hand, I know I've been reaching toward Elle. She stays with me until I completely pass out. I lose my grip on Elle's hand, and my own hand falls to the side of the couch.

The couch turns into nothing but a pitch-black hole. I fall deeper and deeper until I slam onto a hard floor. Now everything's white and shiny. I look around and see a beautiful dress floating in front of me. I get closer to it and see it's made of pale blue silk with lace at the bottom of the sleeves. I reach my hand out to touch it. As soon as the dress and my fingers make contact, a bright flash blinds me. The dress is gone. I turn around to find it and feel the weight of the dress as it clings to my body. I look at myself and twirl around to watch it float around me.

Ash comes out of nowhere wearing a black tux with a white tie. He stops in front of me, and Liam comes out. He is wearing a T-shirt with dark jeans. Liam glares at me and says "Why don't you just go with your new boyfriend?" He turns away from me and walks away.

"I didn't hit him because he's your friend," Ash says as he walks away with Liam.

I try to run to catch up with them, but my legs are numb and hard to control. I just fall to the ground and start crying.

The dress disappears, and I'm back in my old clothes. I wake with a jolt. I feel my face, and tears are still running down my cheeks. I try to stop them, but it takes a while to convince myself that it was just a dream.

When I do, I stop crying, and my head throbs. "Liam!" I call as loud as I can. I look out the window, and it's dark. He must be sleeping, but I don't care. "Liam!" I scream, but no one comes. I start to cry again.

My hearing is starting to come back, and my eyesight works perfectly now. I glance at a small clock above the couch. It reads 5:57. I've been asleep since yesterday afternoon. My stomach grumbles, and I cover it with my hand that Elle held before I passed out. I realize that I haven't eaten anything other than the lemon Liam gave me. It's okay; it's not the first time I've gone a couple days without food.

I stand up and am thankful to find that my legs work properly. I grab a pencil and a small piece of paper and scribble a note that says that I'll be in the woods. I set it down where I was laying and walk out the front door. I close it gently, trying not to wake anyone. I run as fast as I can until I reach the edge of the woods.

I start to slow down because my legs are starting to ache. It doesn't hurt that much, so I just keep on going. I walk instead of run, because I want to enjoy the beauty of the woods. I hear the birds starting to sing, and the peak of the sun catches my eye.

I make it over to Ash's river and sit down on a rock to watch the sun rise. I love the wonderful combinations of all shades of yellows, oranges, pinks, and reds. I really like the reds; in fact, red is my favorite color. I like the deep reds, not the light ones. The color I hate the most is pink, which, of course, is the color most girls wear in school. I don't own one pink piece of clothing. Once I had to wear a pink dress on the first day of school, and pink ribbons in two pigtails held up my hair. My mother said I looked adorable, but I hated it. The only thing on me that wasn't pink was my white shoes. I really liked those shoes; I would love to hear them clank against the floor when I walked.

The mosquitoes are swarming me, searching for a bloody meal. I feel a tiny pain in my arm but it quickly turns to an itch. I don't scratch the mosquito bite; it will just turn into an ugly scar.

I stand up and walk over to a small oak tree and take off my shoes and socks. I set them next to the trunk. A stick breaks in the distance. I whip around and look to see what made the noise. I drop down into the leaves and push them away, hoping to find a sharp stick or a rock. After hearing more breaking sticks, I desperately search the pile of leaves until I feel a slight stabbing pain in my hand. I jerk my hand up and reach down again with caution until I grasp the sharp object. I pull it out of the leaves and see that it's the knife I lost when I was swimming yesterday.

The noise gets nearer until I sense someone standing behind me. I turn quickly and lower my knife when I see Ash. "You shouldn't sneak up on people," I say holding my knife in his view. "Why didn't you tell me that I dropped my knife here?" I ask.

He sits down and rubs his neck. "I don't know," he says and drops his hand to his side.

"I always carry it with me, especially when Liam is angry," I say and put the small blade back in my boot.

"So you would actually stab him with that thing?" Ash asks in shock.

I nod. "Only when he gets out of control. Of course I wouldn't kill him, only injure him enough so I could escape the situation," I say and jump in the water. It isn't as warm as yesterday, and it sends shivers through me.

"You never told me," Ash says as he takes off his shoes, "how old *you* are." He finishes, takes his socks and shirt off, and jumps in.

"Fifteen," I reply when he comes to the surface.

"Cool," he says and floats on his back.

"How come I hardly see you at school?" he asks.

I squint at the bright sun peeking over the horizon. "I don't know; I show up most of the time when me and Elle are feeling okay," I say.

Ash flips over on his stomach and swims around me. "Doesn't your mother take care of you guys?" he asks and stops swimming.

"No," I say trying to sound like I don't care. I try to push thoughts of her out of my mind. I don't know why it bothers me, probably because I haven't talked about her in so long. "When I was ten and Elle was four, my mother ran off one day and my father took off after her. I guess they never really wanted kids so they just left us behind. I guess they assumed our Aunt Lila would take care of us. Aunt Lila is my mother's younger sister. She doesn't like that she has to watch out for us. About twice a month she stops by to see if we need anything and gives us some money to buy food. She never wanted children, so I think we are a burden to her." My voice drops to a whisper. "Only Liam knows my parents left. Elle doesn't even know; she thinks they died." I hit the water with my fist. "I wish they did!" My voice grows loud once more.

Ash grabs my hand when I try to hit the water again. "Now you know something about me," I say and lug my wet body out of the water. My shirt and pants are soaked, but I don't care. I grab my socks and yank them on one by one.

I reach for my boots; pull out my knife and quickly slip my boots back on. Ash puts his hand on my shoulder. "I'm sorry," he says and walks away. I sit there resting my chin on my knee, burrowing the blade of my knife into the dirt. Minutes pass before I remember Ash and run after him.

"Ash!" I call. He doesn't respond. "Ash! Come on!" I scream. "Ash! Where are you?" I turn around looking for any sign of him.

I feel a pair of arms grab me and I scream and thrash around. The person releases me, and I whip around to find Ash rolling around on the ground laughing his head off.

"That wasn't funny! Shut up! I could have stabbed you!" I yell at him.

"Come on! It was funny!" he says and imitates my face. "You looked like you were about to pass out!" he says in between laughs. I huff and walk away. "Serena, why don't you ever laugh?" he says, catching up to me.

"I was dealt a bad hand in life, so excuse me if I'm bitter!" I yell. I'm still clutching the knife. Ash reads my thoughts and grabs the knife before I can do anything.

"Is that really your first resort?" he questions me.

I roll my eyes and turn away from him. "I'll do whatever it takes," I say and sprint for home. I hear Ash trying to keep up with me, but he stumbles and falls behind.

I find myself getting upset the more I think about being alone. I miss my parents. I feel the pressure of raising my little sister alone. I need my mother to help me. I need her to help me with Elle. I need her to protect me. I need her to give me advice on boys. My mind drifts back to Ash.

Why am I going to the dance with Ash? I wonder to myself. *Oh that's right; because I don't want to go with Liam; he's so unpredictable.*

I smile to myself as I visualize the girls at school seeing me with Ash at the dance. They're going to be so jealous! Not that I have feelings for Ash; at least I don't think I do. But everyone is expecting me to show up with Liam. I can see it now, I'm wearing a long, white dress standing next to Ash and all the girls are wondering why Ash picked me instead of Victoria.

Suddenly, I remember what Liam said yesterday—the dance was in two days. So the dance is tomorrow!

I see my house just ahead. I don't stop running until I'm inside. "Elle! If you need me I'll be in the extra room!" I yell. We don't really have an extra room; it was our mom and dad's bedroom. I rip open the closet and admire all of the gorgeous dresses. My mother was beautiful. My dad used to tell me I had her brown eyes and long brown hair. As I rummage through her clothes I see an emerald green dress with a big bow in the front. I grab it, and stare at it. I try to picture my mother wearing this dress. I set it back inside and pull out another. This one is a long, white silk dress with a diamond underneath the chest and a small bow in the back. It's prettied to perfection, as the bottom flows out and the edges are covered in sequins. I immediately slip out of my clothes and gently pull the dress over my head. I look in the mirror and when I do, I see my mother staring back at me.

As I stand in front of the mirror staring at myself, I never realized how much I resemble her. I twirl around to watch the dress float around me. This is the perfect dress, I decide and carefully take it off and lay it neatly on the bed. I put on a blue shirt and jeans. I run my hand over the dress to feel the silky material. Then it dawns on me: What will Elle wear?

I pull open the closet and search for a small enough dress to fit her. I look at the dark blue, cotton dress with sleeves made of white lace. *Too big.* I pull out a short, red one with long, flowing sleeves. *Still too big.* I spot a purple dress with no sleeves that's covered in glitter. I think Elle will like the purple one. I grab it and call for her. She runs into the room and her eyes light up when she sees the dress.

"I was thinking maybe you would like to wear this dress at the dance," I say. Elle gives me a big hug, grabs the dress from my hands, and runs in my room to try it on. She is out in less than a minute wearing the dress. I am stunned by how beautiful she looks and how well it fits her.

"What do you think?" she asks, turning for me.

"I think you look beautiful," I say as I ruffle her hair. She giggles and runs back in to change out of it.

"So, who are you going with?" I ask her when she appears again.

"I don't have a date for the dance. I'm meeting some of my friends there," she says excitedly and walks out of the room but quickly pops back in. "Are you still going with Ash? If you weren't, I so would!" she adds sarcastically.

I grab my wet clothes and walk outside to lay them across the porch to dry. I hear a noise and turn around to see Ash leaning against the house. "Oh jeez; you scared me!" I say, and he smiles. I take his hand. "Come here; I want to show you something." I say and he follows. I lead him into the extra room and show him the dress.

"It's amazing," he gasps and sits on the bed.

"Thanks, it's my mother's dress. Well… it was her dress," I say and put it back in the closet. I sit down next to Ash. I don't know what came over me, but I start laughing.

He looks at me like I'm crazy. "You're actually laughing?" he asks sarcastically.

"I guess I am," I reply. "What are you going to wear to the dance?" I ask him.

"Most likely a white suit with a tie."

"Bow tie," I say.

"Okay, I'll wear a bow tie," he says.

"I'm thirsty," I say and get up. "I'll get some water. Want any?"

"No thanks," he says. I smile and walk out of the room.

As I enter the kitchen I see Liam standing there. I jump. "God! Why is everybody sneaking up on me today?" I ask.

He shrugs, walks over to a cupboard, and pulls out two plastic glasses. He then walks over to the tiny fridge and pulls out a jug of water. He pours the water into the cups and hands them to me. The water is warm, but it's no surprise, because our fridge doesn't work well.

"How did you—" I start to ask, but Liam cuts me off.

"I overheard you guys. So you found a dress? Hmm?" He asks.

I feel very uncomfortable and shift my feet. "Um, yeah. Want to see it?" I ask. He nods and follows me to the room. I hesitate before entering the extra room, but when I do, Ash jumps to his feet when he sees Liam.

I hand him a glass, and he takes it. I set my own glass on a bedside table and walk towards the closet. "Why is he shirtless?" Liam asks.

"We went swimming," I say, not turning around. I didn't even notice that Ash hadn't put his shirt back on. I feel kind of stupid now for not realizing it before.

I open the closet door and grab the dress. I pivot on my heel and face them.

"Impressive," he says after taking it out of my hand,

looking at it as he turns it every which way to get a better look at it.

"Thanks. Hey, Liam, why were you in my house in the first place?" I ask him.

He gives the dress back to me. "I saw the note you left and decided to come over here to check on you, because I knew you wouldn't come back to my house," he answers. I admit, he knows me too well, but don't say anything.

"Who are you taking to the dance?" Ash asks Liam. I can tell Liam is annoyed with Ash. He answers through clenched teeth, "I'm taking Victoria Glass."

Ash chokes on his water and some of it sprays out of his mouth. "Victoria Glass?!" he repeats. "Isn't she that really rich red head who is in love with every guy she sees?" Ash laughs.

I can tell that Liam is trying to control his temper. "Yes. She begged me to take her and since I didn't have anyone to go with, I had to say yes."

I can't help it; I laugh to myself. Is it funny? Yes! Is it sad that Liam was stuck taking Victoria? Yes. I feel bad for him because I know he wanted me to go with him.

"Victoria even told me what she is going to wear!" Liam says, disgusted.

"What is she wearing?" I ask trying to hold back the laughter. I take a sip of water, so I have something else to do with my mouth other than laugh.

"A pink, sleeveless mini dress with giant red heels," he says, rolling his eyes.

I can't help it; I laugh so hard and the water spits out of my mouth. "Oh my God!" I shout. "Is she really wearing pink? Didn't she wear that for picture day, and it made her look ridiculous?" I ask, and Ash nods. Liam face turns bright red. I can't tell if it's from embarrassment or from being so mad at Ash and me for laughing. "We're sorry," I say and put my hand on his arm. "But it's so freaking hilarious!" Ash blurts out and continues laughing.

Liam walks out the door and turns around. "If only you knew what I know, you would pick me over him instantly," he turns back around and walks out of the room.

I run after him. "What are you talking about?" I shout to him, "Why are you talking nonsense?"

He stops, turns around and reminds me what I said. "You said yourself that we're just friends. Just leave it at that."

I can feel rage building up inside me. "Liam Nelson, get back here now!" I scream. Ash stops laughing and I hear Liam slam the front door. I run to the door and grab the door knob. I stand there, frozen, unable to find enough mental strength to open it.

Instead, I lean against the door with my back and drop to the floor and put my head on my knees. Ash runs from the bedroom and drops down next to me. I don't want his comfort, but I don't resist when he puts my head on his shoulder. I stop complaining about Liam after about a minute and stand up. Ash stays on the ground and looks up at me. I walk a few steps when my ankle gives way dropping me back onto the hard floor. I don't bother getting up this time.

Ash can tell by the look on my face that I'm not hurt. He reaches out to help me, but I shrug him off. He gets to his feet and leaves me lying there. Elle hears the commotion and rushes to my side. She wraps her small arms around me and looks at me with those big brown eyes. "I can tell Liam likes you. I mean, *really* likes you even though you screamed at him. Maybe you need to spend some time apart," she whispers and hugs me tighter. "Be careful Serena, I think Ash likes you too."

"I know," I whisper back.

CHAPTER 2

I thought about how long Ash and I have known each other. *Two days. Only that long?* It feels longer. But no, I count the days on my fingers again. *Only two.* I count the years that Liam and I have known each other. *Five.* Liam has been supporting me as a friend from the first day my parents ran off. We've always been close friends, but sometimes I think he wants to be more than friends. *Maybe he's waiting for me to discover that on my own. Or am I reading him all wrong? Maybe he wants to be just friends.* My thoughts are broken when Elle pulls back from me and walks away.

I pull myself up, walk to my bedroom and drop on the bed face first. I hate that Liam and I are fighting over a school dance. How lame!

Elle calls to me about her going to the woods for a quick walk. She doesn't need my okay, but she likes to inform me anyway. I hear the door open and close.

I try to release the stress by punching my pillow and amazingly I feel much better after I'm done. *Is this how Liam feels when he gets rid of his anger and stress?* I think about this and decide it must help relieve *some* stress, because yesterday at the river Liam unleashed his anger on Ash. *Why did Liam hit Ash? Was it because he was jealous? Or was it something else that made him mad?* I rub the spot on my head where Liam hit me.

Ash is muscular and strong, but when he's confronted he doesn't take action and become violent like Liam. He walks away instead of fighting. I'm the opposite. I'll fight anyone unless it's Liam, then I run. He gets so angry and lashes out. I'm not sure what he is capable of, but I don't want to find out. In the fifth grade, I saw him break a boy's arm because he was flirting with me. If he could do that back then, I'm sure he can snap a person's neck if someone provoked him. But the sad thing is I can actually see him hurting me and I'm his closest friend. I'm more worried for Ash than me, though, because Liam holds grudges. After the dance, I'll be sure to leave my knife with Ash.

I roll over on my back and stare at the ceiling, thinking about nothing in particular. I fall asleep, and I'm back in the fantasy gown. But this time, I'm dancing with Ash, and Liam is dancing with Victoria. Those are the only people I recognize in the crowd. When the song ends, Ash walks away from me and gets lost in the sea of people. No matter how many people I push through, he is never there. I call out his name, but he doesn't come.

I run back to Liam, but he's gone also. Victoria just stands there, mouth open wide, dark blood dripping from her arm. I see my knife on the floor with her blood on it. She smiles at me and disappears. I hear a scream that belongs to Elle. I run and shove my way through the crowd to reach her, but I find her being taken by Victoria. I try to grab her, but I can't reach Elle.

I open my eyes and feel my heart. It's pounding, and I'm sweating. I sit up and call for Elle. Emptiness is all that calls back from the house. How long did I sleep? I get up and pull my boots on. I run for the door and rip it open and slam it shut. I feel rain on my skin and look up. Gray, fluffy clouds are forming over the town.

"Elle!" I scream. I head for the woods. "Elle!" I shriek again and again; still no response. I run into the woods, and I'm sheltered from the rain by the trees. "Elle! Elle, its Serena!" I shout.

A tiny voice comes from the distance. "Serena!" she yells.

I run in the direction of her voice. "Elle! Where are you?" I scream. I reach for my knife. It's not there. "Elle! Elle I'm coming!" I shriek. I pick up speed and charge through the woods.

"Serena!" she calls again, but her voice is faint and muffled. I come to where she lies; her shirt is torn and bloody, and her pants are ripped. I see a small, scraggly wolf scurrying away. I pick up a pointed stick six yards from my foot and run after it. It's fast, but I see the wolf limping; his back paw appears to be injured and I catch it before it can run very far.

I pierce its back with the stick, and watch the wolf stumble and collapse onto its side. I stand there watching it—blood is pouring out around the stick and onto the ground where it laid. It moves a little and tries to get away, but it is held captive by the stick, and it falls to the ground a bloody mess.

I run back to Elle; she is crying. I look over her wounds. They aren't as bad as I would have thought until I see the top of her right hand. I see a deep, bloody gash right above her wrist and hope it didn't puncture the vein. I'm shocked by the sight of the hole in her arm and I rip a piece of her torn pants and wrap it tightly to stop the bleeding.

"Don't worry," attempting to comfort her, "I'll clean you up, and you'll be alright." I pick her up and carry her all the way home.

I set her on the couch and get a wet towel to clean up her smaller wounds first. I save the big one for last. I remove the bloody cloth from her wrist and gently wipe away the blood. I put some peroxide on it and watch it bubble and foam out of the cut. I wash it out with water and put more and more peroxide on it until it stops bubbling. I wrap a clean towel around her wrist in hopes that the wound won't get infected.

I hear the door open, and Liam walks in. He sees Elle and rushes over to help. He grabs a wet cloth from the table and tries to soothe her with Pine Hill fantasy stories about a brother and sister who went walking through the woods one day and found a golden tree or something. I don't really pay attention. I'm trying not to cry when Liam gently reaches over and rubs my back. I don't look up from Elle's face to acknowledge his act of kindness.

Liam continues with his Pine Hill story until Elle closes her eyes and falls asleep. Finally, I look at Liam and try to smile. "Thanks," I whisper, being careful not to wake Elle.

"You're welcome," Liam whispers back.

"You need to explain why I would choose you," I say softly.

He shifts uncomfortably in a chair and looks at his

feet. "Nothing, just um," he stumbles to find the right words. If I knew what he was going to say, I would help him, but I have no clue how to. "I'm glad you got a date to the dance," he finally says.

I smile. "That was your big change-Serena's-mind-about-you thought?" I ask him.

He shrugs. "No, but I don't know how to explain it. Plus, I'm not allowed to tell you...yet," he says. "You'll find out soon enough."

I try to make sense of what he just was trying to tell me, but forget about it. "You know, I would like to go with you to the dance, but we would just go as friends," I say and put my hand on his shoulder.

"Yeah, you tell me that now!" he says and takes my hand off. I look at my feet.

"Why did you hit Ash yesterday?" I ask him.

He stares straight ahead as if he were trying to remember something. "Do you remember when Logan Owens asked you out in fifth grade?"

I laugh quietly. "Yeah, and you broke his arm for it!" I say, poking his stomach.

He turns to me and smiles. "Yep, that's the one. Anyway, I feel the need to protect you in sort of a brotherly way," he says.

I frown. "But now you feel differently," I say while I twist my hair in between my fingers.

"No. I mean, yes. I mean, kind of. You know that I've always liked you," he says and looks at the floor again.

"No, actually I didn't know that; I mean, I knew you liked me a couple days ago, but back then? When you first met me?"

"Even before then," he cuts the conversation short and

stands up. "I hope Elle feels better." he walks away from me to avoid answering any more questions.

I watch Liam standing quietly in the other room debating whether or not he should leave. I don't know why he stays around. He reaches for the door knob and without turning away, he says, "Later," and walks out of the house. I follow him outside, but he's already gone. I look up to see the rain has stopped, and the sun has come out.

I decide I need to pick up some groceries, so I pull out the change jar and unscrew the cap. I take out the last of the coins. I run to the market and buy some carrots, a stick of butter, and two apples. I carry them back in a small, brown paper bag. I'm not far from my house when I run into Ash—literally run into him. We hit heads, and the food inside the bag tumbles to the ground.

I rub my head, and Ash does the same. "Ow!" I shriek and quickly collect the scattered groceries. Ash is gathering the apples as I scramble for the carrots and butter. *There's a first time for everything,* I think and hold out the bag so he can drop in the bruised apples. We both regain our standing positions, and he brushes off some of the dirt on my shirt.

"I'm so sorry about that!" he says as he brushes his own clothes off now.

"Me too," I say and refuse his offer to carry the bag. "Elle refuses to eat, so I'm going to make her favorite dish and see if she will eat," I explain before turning to walk away. Ash catches up with me and turns me around.

"What happened to Elle?" he asks with eyes wide and concerned.

"Nothing," I say and try to turn around again, but

Ash's hold is too strong. "Fine! She was attacked by a small wolf," I blurt out.

Ash gasps. "What?" He releases my shoulders. "Where did this happen?" Ash asks in shock. I don't answer and turn to run, and Ash runs after me.

When we reach the house, I open the door and run inside, not bothering to close it since Ash is close behind. I empty the bag of groceries and start chopping the apples in small chunks. I take whatever honey we have and mix the apples, honey, and butter together in a small pan and put it on the stove to cook. I glance up to see Ash sitting next to Elle, being careful not to wake her. I grab a large wooden spoon and stir the ingredients together until it is mixed well and warm to the touch. I pour it on a plate and carry it to where Elle is laying.

"Wake her up," I whisper to him.

"Why?" he whispers back.

"Because, she would love to see your face first thing after she wakes up," I say and nudge him. He sighs and gently shakes Elle. "Elle, wake up," he says until her eyes open. It doesn't take much to persuade her to eat the honey, butter, and apple mixture. After she finishes eating the last bite, I stroke her hair until she falls asleep. Ash just sits there, silent and stiff.

"What do your parents do for work?" I ask him.

"Nothing much I guess, just getting by each day with hunting and raising chickens," he chuckles. "I sometimes give swim lessons."

"That's cool," I say, although I don't mean it. Lakes, rivers, and waterfalls surround our town. I learned how to swim when I was young, like most of the people in our town.

"I can swim fine," I say and start braiding my hair. I hate ponytails. They are always loose and in the way; braids are tight and out of the way. It takes me no time at all to finish it. I look at the clock. "Nine fifty-two," I whisper aloud.

"What?" Ash asks me.

I help get him to his feet. "It's late; go get some sleep. I'll see you tomorrow," I say and push him out the door.

"Night!" he says.

"Night," I mumble back and close the door.

I walk back to where Elle is sleeping and pick her up and carry her to her bed and pull the covers over her. She lies there with a half smile on her face. Her face is the only place on her body that the wolf didn't bite or scratch. I grab the purple dress and set it next to her. I smooth it out nice and neat before I leave. I walk back to my room and flop on the bed. With everything that happened today, it didn't take long before I was fast asleep.

In the morning, I lie in bed with my eyes closed. I realize I didn't have a bad dream last night.

I finally open my eyes and crawl out of bed. Morning comes so quickly and I feel like my mind and body are moving in slow motion. I shuffle my feet across the hardwood floor until I reach the kitchen. I look at the clock and it reads 5:47. I shuffle back to Elle's room to wake her up. I shake her lightly. "Elle! Elle, time to go to school!" I softly whisper.

Her eyes flutter open and she looks around. She stumbles out of bed; I think it's cute to watch her sleepy little body stretching to wake up. She walks to her closet and pulls out a blue plaid shirt with long shorts.

I walk back to my room and get dressed in there. I

pull on a plain green shirt and slip on a pair of mid-thigh shorts. I walk to the bathroom, and find Elle brushing her hair. I go down to the kitchen, cut up some carrots, and pour two glasses of water for breakfast. "Elle!" I call to her.

"Yeah," she yells back.

"Breakfast is ready!" I say. Elle rushes down; her hair is smoothed back and shiny. I've always envied her light, beautiful brown hair, whereas mine is dark brown and only sometimes (if I wash it a ton) shiny. I sit down to eat with Elle.

We finish our carrots in no time and drink our water. I go upstairs and brush my hair with the same brush that Elle used. Elle comes back up and brushes her teeth with me. We have no running water, and our pump works sometimes and sometimes it doesn't, so we keep a bucket outside to catch rainfall for extra water.

We spit into a small sink, wipe our faces off on a nearby cloth, and pull on our shoes and socks. We each have a small book bag provided by the school to carry our books, homework, and lunch in. But since we don't have lunch, our bag is a little bit lighter than everyone else's bag.

Before I leave, I find my knife sitting on the floor and pick it up. I open the front zipper on my bag and put it in, stuffing it all the way down so it won't fall out. I zip it back up and rush downstairs and find Elle at the door. "Ready?" I ask her.

"Yep!" she confirms and looks in her bag again to make sure she has everything.

"You look like you're feeling better today," I say with a small laugh and guide her out the door.

When we reach the school yard, Elle squeals and points. "That's who I'm going to the dance with!" she says. I look over in that direction and see a cute boy with black hair, blue eyes, and a nice smile. Elle never mentioned she was going with someone. I'm a little disappointed she didn't confide in me.

"I thought you said you were going with friends. Are you boyfriend and girlfriend?" I tease her.

She frowns. "No, we're just friends." she says and sighs. I watch her as she walks away to find her friends. She turns and waves good-bye to me, and I wave back.

"Serena!" I hear someone call my name, and I look around. "Serena!" I hear again. Ash steps out from a crowd of people.

"Hey, Ash," I call back. I quickly glance at a group of girls and can see them whisper and point in my direction. I don't care; I never cared what they thought about me.

"Are you still wearing that dress?" he asks me, and I nod. "Cool," he says. Out of the corner of my eye I see Victoria waiving her hand in the air.

"Ash!" she calls.

He just stands there without turning around and huffs. "Is that Victoria?" he asks. I nod again, and he sighs.

"Ash!" she calls again. Not only is Victoria insanely annoying, she sometimes stalks the cute guys in school. Some guys think it's cool when she flirts with them. But once they get to know her, it doesn't take long before you see them trying to avoid her.

I'm pretty sure Victoria's friends think I'm jealous of her. Maybe I'm jealous of her boldness to go after what she wants, even if it doesn't want her. I look toward Victoria and shout, "What do you want?" I see her mouth drop open and her blue eyes bulge out wide.

"What?!" she yells at me. Victoria pushes her way in between me and Ash. "I said what do you want? Have some self-respect, but obviously you don't have any, at least respect other people!" I spew out the words at the back of her head.

Victoria turns around to face me. She is within inches of my face. "Do you know who you're messing with?" she asks me in a sassy tone. I wipe the spit from my eye that she sprayed when she talked.

"Yeah, I'm dealing with a girl who still doesn't know how to talk without spitting," I challenge her. She gives me a slight nudge and I step back and smile. This is not going to end well I think to myself.

I see people starting to gather around us. I guess I've pushed Victoria to the edge because she launches at me with an open hand to smack my face. I grab her hand before it strikes and tighten my grip on it until she shakes me off. She glares at me and then looks down to see three of her sparkly pink manicured fingernails are broken to the nub, and her hand is lightly dripping blood from where I jabbed her skin with my own nail. I can see tears welling up in her eyes, and she whips around and pushes through the crowd to get away from me.

Ash comes up from behind me and grabs my wrist. "Come on, let's go," he whispers and rushes me out of there. I can hear people laughing and cheering.

It's difficult to focus on school today. Time seems to be dragging slowly. The only satisfying moment I have is from Victoria giving me dirty looks as I pass her throughout the day. The bell rings and history class is finally over. We are allowed a five-minute break in between each class. I head to my locker and turn the combination from eight to zero to twenty-four. The locker pops open, and I put my history books and notebooks inside it. I grab my writing notebooks and pull out my textbook and close my locker. I start to walk away, but someone slams into my left shoulder.

I fall to the ground, and all of my notebooks scatter. I look up to see who pushed me and see Victoria laughing with her friends. "Oops. Sorry, Serena; I kind of tripped." She adds air quotes when she says "tripped."

As I gather my things, I look up to see Victoria moving towards her friends. I stand up and walk over to where they are laughing and pointing at me. Two of the girls scatter when they see me coming, but the other three girls move in closer to Victoria. "You've got real nerve to push Vic around like that," a girl with red hair and blue eyes starts to say before I cut her off.

"Shut up!" I tell her. I get really close to Victoria's face. "You can treat me like dirt, but I'm warning you! I poke her really hard in the chest. You better not treat Liam like crap at the dance!" I assert and take a step back.

She smirks. "And what if I do?" she barks back at me.

I take a step closer to her and dig my finger into her chest. "If you do, then you will have to deal with more than a few broken nails," the words coming out through clenched teeth. I whip around, not sure if she was going to attack me from behind. I hear her huff and stomp away.

Once I'm in the classroom seated, I soon realize that I made a big mistake—Victoria knows my weakness. She knows that Liam means a lot to me and she can use that to her advantage. I don't have the right to ask Liam to take someone else to the dance. Someone! Anyone, but Victoria! I ruined that opportunity by rejecting his offer. I know Liam doesn't like Victoria the same way he likes me, but will I be able to watch them together? Will Liam be able to control his temper with Victoria if she says the wrong thing? All of these questions fill my head until the teacher calls on me.

"Serena, would you like to read your homework story out loud?" Mr. Swanson says. He is my favorite teacher, but sometimes he can call on me at the wrong time.

"Um, sure," I stutter and pull out my homework.

"Now, did you do a fairytale or something that has happened to you?" he asks me.

"Something that has happened to me," I say and begin reading.

"Terrified, I climb into a tree. He tries to climb it, but he can't make it as far up as me and goes down. I try to climb higher, but when I try to hold onto the branch above me, it snaps—I am trapped there. I hear him mutter something under his breath, but I can't understand it. All I know is that this is the only place safe for me now." I finish and everyone is quiet, even Mr. Swanson has to take a second to snap back into real life.

"Well, that sure was intense," he says. Some kids nod in agreement. "Serena, who was 'he'?" Mr. Swanson asks. I can tell the rest of the class wants to know too.

"I'm sorry. I can't share that," I say. Everyone looks disappointed, even Victoria.

"I'm sorry, Serena, but in order to write a complete story, you must give all of the characters' names." I can tell he really wants to know who I was writing about, but I refuse to sell Liam out.

"I'm sorry, Mr. Swanson. I cannot share that," I say more firmly this time.

He frowns. "Okay, Miss Coleman, I understand," he says and writes my grade in his grade book.

"Thank you," I tell him and take my seat.

Mr. Swanson doesn't call on me for the rest of the hour, and I'm grateful.

The bell rings, and we are let out of class. As soon as I'm in the hallway, everyone swarms me, begging to know who "he" was. I tell them sorry and walk away. Eventually everyone realizes I'm not going to spill my guts and they leave me alone. I sling my book bag over my shoulder and slam my locker. Victoria comes up to me.

"I want to say I'm sorry for the way I acted and was wondering if you'd like to be friends? I mean, I'm popular; you're popular. Everyone will expect us to be friends, right?" she says.

"Since when am I popular?" I ask. She holds her hand out for me to shake. "No," I say and walk away. I don't trust her.

I run into Liam in the hall after he finishes gym class. "I heard you and Victoria got into a fight. What about?" he asks while we walk together.

"Nothing important. Just that she was bothering Ash and wouldn't shut up, so I kind of got in her face," I say with my head down.

We reach the boys locker room, and he stops. "Sweet! I didn't know you had it in you. Did she attack you?"

I smile. "What do you think? She started to slap me, so I grabbed her hand and it was over," I say, almost laughing. Liam laughs a little and walks into the locker room. A few other guys pass by me staring and smiling.

I feel weird, so I start walking quickly in the opposite direction.

I see Elle and call her name. She is laughing with a couple other girls but tells them good-bye and runs over to me. I hug her, and she hugs me back. "Come on," I tell her. "Let's go home and get changed."

She nods excitedly and rushes me out the door. "Some kids asked me about all of the scratches I had, and I told them I got attacked by a wolf. They didn't believe me, though," she says looking over her wounds.

CHAPTER 3

When we get home, Elle runs to her room to get ready for the dance. I laugh to myself and go into my room to change into my dress. I take out my mother's makeup out of the top shelf of the cupboard in her bedroom and open it. Slightly used mascara, hardly touched eyeliner, ten types of lipsticks and lip glosses, blush, brushes, and eye shadow. I yell for Elle, and she joins me.

I sit her down and look at her perfect face. I brush the pale pink blush on her cheekbones. I do her eyes next with tan color eye shadow, careful not to get makeup in her eye. Finally, I put a touch of pink lipstick on her soft lips. Elle admires herself in the mirror.

I take the mirror from Elle and look at my tired eyes. I apply black eyeliner on the top and bottom of my eyes, the peach color blush to match my cheeks, and deep pink for my lips. The lipstick isn't dark; it's just a really rich shade. I put the finishing touch on my eye lids using a silver eye shadow. I look at myself in the mirror. I turn around to get the full view of my dress.

Elle tugs on my arm. "Come on! We'll be late!" she

whines. We put on our shoes—Elle has sparkly black flats, and I have silver heels that my mother used to wear.

We arrive at the school and hear loud music pouring out of the building. We get inside to see that all of the girls are in beautiful dresses, and most of them are different shades of pink. The boys are in either suits or black or white vests with dress pants.

I look around for Ash while Elle searches around for her friends. She spots her girlfriends and takes off. "Hey," I hear someone's voice behind me. It's Liam in a midnight blue suit. "Does this suit make me look fat?" he jokes.

I laugh. "No, you look fine," I say.

He thanks me and compliments me on my dress. "It looks even better on you than on the hanger," he tells me. I'm starting to feel a little jealous of Ash.

Victoria walks up to him and grabs his arm. "Time to dance!" she says and waves good-bye with her fingers at me. Victoria and Liam leave me standing there alone.

I feel a tap on my shoulder and turn around. This time, it's Ash. "Hey, Ash, nice suit. You even remembered the bowtie," I say and grab his tie with both hands to straighten it.

"Yeah, do you like it?" he asks turning for me.

"Yes! It's amazing!" I say.

He smiles. "Let's go," he says, and we walk out to the gym where everyone is dancing. Everyone looks like they are having a great time dancing and chatting. I'm glad it's an upbeat song, because I don't feel comfortable slow dancing with Ash. We just stand next to each other and talk most of the time. I catch a glimpse of Elle with her friends, and they look like they're having a good time dancing. They put on a slow song, and I feel my stomach churning. I can tell Ash is nervous too because he starts looking around and tapping his foot. I try to give us both a way out so I say, "Um, I'm going to go to the bathroom," and quickly walk to the bathroom.

I might as well fix my hair when I'm in here so I do something constructive, I think and smooth my hair down in front of the mirror. When the song is almost over, I go back out. The song is over by the time I reach Ash, and an up-beat song is playing again. "Sorry I took so long," I say.

"I know you felt awkward when that song came on. I sort of was too," he admits, and I nod my head. "Don't worry; it's fine," he assures me.

I feel weird inside, though, like little butterflies are flying around in my stomach but at the same time gnawing at me. I can't help it; I laugh. Ash looks at me like I'm crazy. "What?" he asks.

"Nothing. There's just this weird feeling inside my stomach like gnawing butterflies or something," I say and laugh again. I'm glad that no one is paying attention to us, but then I realize there is. I look to my right and see Liam staring at us. My face turns red, and I drag Ash somewhere else to dance. After two fast songs later another slow song starts playing.

Ash and I don't look at each other for about thirty seconds of the song, and finally he reaches out and gently touches the back of my hand. I hesitate at first, but take it. He curls his fingers around mine and he walks me out of the gym. "What?" I ask him when I notice we are headed away from the dance floor.

"I don't feel too good," he says.

"What's wrong?" I ask.

"Nothing. There's just this weird feeling inside my

stomach like gnawing butterflies or something," he says smiling.

I smile back. "Very funny," I say sarcastically. "Let's get back before Liam starts looking for me."

Ash tugs at my hand. "I want to show you something," he says as he pulls me down the hall.

He opens the music room door, and looks around to see if anyone is in there. He leads me to the wooden piano and sits down. He taps the bench to motion for me to sit next to him. I sit next to him and watch as he starts playing a song that is very familiar to me, but I can't remember the lyrics. He starts humming the lyrics, and I remember now.

I begin to sing. It was a song we sang in first and second grade. "See the passing birds go by and the white clouds in the sky. It's a beautiful spring day after a warm soft rain. The small pink flowers, the minutes in an hour." I stop singing and Ash stops humming. "I never got that part—the minutes in an hour. It doesn't make sense to me," I say.

Ash wraps up with a few extra notes on the piano. "Me either," he adds. He points to the piano. "Want to try?" he asks me. I shake my head no, but he takes my hands and places them on the keys. "This is C, this is D, this is E, this is, F, and this is G." He points to each key as he says the letters.

"Okay," I say and press D. I press D, C, F, and G. It doesn't sound as nice as I thought it should, so I keep trying. Ash stops me on my fourth attempt and shows me two other notes: A and B. I ask what the black keys do, and he tells me that they are either flats or sharps. He plays E and drops down to the black key. "That is E flat," he explains and then puts his fingers on D. "This is D sharp," he explains again, striking the black key next to it.

"Okay," I say and hit the keys. I play them in the order of C, E, G, F, and D over and over again. I hold down one of the petals, which makes the music come together. "It's wonderful," I whisper.

"Thanks," he whispers back.

I hear the door open, and we quickly stand up, knocking the bench over. Ash and I try to pick it up at the same time, and our heads collide. "Ouch!" I yell. We place the bench back in the upright position. I see Mr. Welch, the music teacher, gasping as he sees us on *his* piano. He is my least favorite teacher (and the meanest).

"What is going on here?" he yells at us.

"You see, Mr. Welch," Ash starts, but I stop him by putting my hand over his mouth. We look at each other and as if we silently communicated with each other, we run for the door and into the hallway.

Mr. Welch runs after us. "Stop!" he shouts and holds out his hand to grab us. I'm faster than Ash, so I let him get ahead of me, and I try to cause a diversion and tip the chairs over in the hallway. They end with a thump, and I run to catch up with Ash. When I reach him, we start laughing. "Get back here!" Mr. Welch yells. We ignore him and keep running until we are safe outside the school.

I lean against the brick wall and feel my heart racing. "That was so much fun!" I chuckle.

"Yeah!" Ash agrees.

"That was way better than dancing!" I say.

He nods. "We should do this more often!" Ash says and leans against the wall next to me. I look up at the sky; it's dark and filled with stars.

"It must be around eight o'clock or so," I assume. Ash looks up also. I point to a bright star in front of him. "See that star?" He nods. "That's my lucky star. That's the star I wished on the night my parents left Elle and me. I wished for an angel to help us get through it."

He points to another star next to mine. "That is my lucky star," he says. "I wished on that star the night before I met you."

My mouth goes dry, and I feel the color rush from my face. "What? Wait...what did you wish for?" I ask. He starts to tell me, but I'm not sure if I want to hear it, so I cut him off. I'm glad I did, because Liam and Victoria come walking out of the door. I suddenly get really mad for the intrusion.

"Were you guys spying on us!?" I ask.

Victoria laughs really hard, and I turn to punch her in the face, but Ash stops me. "Not a good idea, you'll stain your dress," he whispers. His hand covers my fist, I shake it off.

"Gosh, Serena, take a chill pill! Not everything is about you!" Victoria snorts and starts laughing again. This time, no one tries to stop me.

I hit her right in the nose as hard as I can. It doesn't seem to phase her and she continues laughing this strange laugh as blood trickles down her lip and over her chin. I curl my fist to hit her again, but Liam and Ash both stop me. Ash gets a hold of my right hand, and Liam grabs the left. Victoria walks away laughing and Ash and Liam are trying to calm me down. Something's not right; I get a flashback of one of my nightmares and scream, "Let me go!" I thrash around trying to free myself.

"Elle!" I scream. I slip out of Liam's grip, but Ash still

holds on tight. I try my hardest to pull away from him, but he doesn't move. I see Victoria go into the school, and I scream, "I have to get Elle!" Ash lets go of my hand. I stumble back for a second but recover before I fall to the ground. I dodge Liam as he tries to grab me again and take off running towards the school to stop Victoria. It wasn't Liam she was planning on hurting.

Even though I have a head start, Liam quickly gains on me. I barely make it inside when he grabs my shoulders and turns me around. "What is wrong with you?" he yells at me.

"I had a nightmare about—" And that's all it takes for Liam to hear and he calls out Elle's name. Liam knows how freaky real my nightmares can get. Ash doesn't understand what's going on, but he calls out to Elle too.

I hear a scream from the back of the crowd and push my way through everyone until I see Elle falling down the wall and Victoria standing over her. My adrenaline kicked in and I jumped Victoria from behind, knocking her against the wall. I pinned her trying to figure out if I should kill her for what she did to Elle or check to see how much damage she did. I dig my nails into her bare shoulders breaking her skin until she screams. Everyone goes silent; they all turn their attention to us, but I don't care.

"What were you doing to my little sister?" I demand.

She throws me off her back and faces me. Her shoulders are covered in blood. She laughs and walks toward Elle who is lying on the floor. Elle starts crying harder and curls up in a ball when she sees Victoria coming towards her. I have to get to Elle first. I run past Victoria, and block her from getting to Elle. As Victoria approaches within inches of me, she smiles wide and I see large sharp teeth.

Liam charges into her and knocks her to the floor, also knocking me to the floor. I get up and see him pinning Victoria against the wall. Her teeth are growing into fangs and her eyes are changing shape. Ash rushes to help Liam stop Victoria. He elbows her in the side of her head and she falls to the ground.

By this time, everyone is running out of the school. "Ash, get the police," I say.

"But I should stay here in case Liam needs my help," he argues.

We don't have time for this! "Ash, go now! The more time we argue, the more time we waste!" I yell at him.

"Fine," he says and gives me a hug. I watch him run out the door.

"This...thing, what do you think it is?" Liam asks me.

"I don't know, but I've dreamt most of what has happened," I say as I notice Victoria's complexion is turning gray and brown. Her eyes turn into little slits, and her nose turns into two small holes. Her mouth is the most freighting thing I've ever seen—long, chapped, black lips hiding daggers for teeth. "I'm going to go find something to tie it down with," I say and leave.

I go out into the hallway and see the art room. I rush inside and gather as much wire as I can carry and bring it back to him I can tell that she is starting to wake up, and I drop the wire at Liam's feet. He picks it up and starts tying her up. I hear her grunt and try to hit her in the side of the head to knock her out again like Ash did, but I fail. Her mouth opens, and I find myself staring at her sharp teeth.

Not knowing what's going to happen to us, I silently say good-bye to Ash and thank him for being my friend even though I never deserved it. I help restrain Victoria; or whatever this is, in the wire. After we are done, I put a hand on Liam's arm. He looks at me and knows what I am thinking. He knows I'm scared; he knows that we will always be friends, and that's all we'll ever be. He takes my hand and stands up. For a second I think he might kiss me, but he doesn't. I stand up as well. Victoria is starting to thrash about.

"Let's go," Liam says looking into my eyes.

"What do we do with her?" as I point to Victoria.

"Just leave her, we are leaving." Liam says and grabs me by the wrist.

"We'll never make it!" I shriek.

"We can try," he says and we run for the door.

After we're safely out of the building, I feel a sense of relief until I remember Elle. "Oh my God! I forgot Elle!" I scream and run back to the school.

Liam grabs my arm. "It's dangerous to go back in Serena," he tries to persuade me.

I pull away from him and run back inside. "Elle!" I scream as loud as I can. "Elle!" I see her stumbling towards me in her torn dress. I run to her and scoop her up in my arms and make my way to the door. Liam finds us and takes Elle from my arms.

We run as fast as we can away from the school. But I stop when I hear a loud screech and remember Ash. He's probably looking for me and Elle.

"I have to go back!" I shout to Liam. "Take Elle somewhere safe and don't leave her side!" I yell and head back to the school. It feels like an eternity by the time I reach the school. There are police cars outside the school with their lights on. Where is everyone? As I approach the police cars I gasp.

"Oh No!" I murmur. I see two police men on the ground, torn to shreds. There are more police taking cover near their cars and around the school. I look past them and see Ash lying on the ground near one of the policemen. I can see him moving around trying to get up. He's covered in blood. "Ash!" I scream and run towards him.

I see this demon creature perched on the roof of the school looking down. It looks like an alien lizard I've seen it in one of my nightmares. "What are you doing? Get out of here!" one of the police men shouts at me.

I turn towards Ash and watch him pull out a knife from the dead police men's side pocket. He throws it near my foot. I reach down and grab it. The demon creature is about five feet tall, has a thin body and large spiky wings. It flies over to me and lands within a few inches of where I'm standing. It laughs the same way as Victoria did earlier.

"Take your best shot!" it sneers.

Out of the corner of my eye, I see Ash in the background pointing at his neck. I move closer to the demon creature and it grabs my arm. I can feel its cold breath in my face.

At that moment I hear a loud bang! The demon stumbles back losing its grip it had on me. I watch as the demon is distracted by the leg wound caused by the bullet. I tighten my grip on the knife and with every ounce of energy I have, I lunge the knife into its neck. It screeches loudly piercing my ears. I watch its sinister skinny fingers grab a hold of the knife sticking out of its neck. It pulls the knife out and drops it in front of me. I want to run, but my legs won't move. It looks back at me and lunges toward me. I close my eyes and think of Elle. When I open my eyes, I see the demon lying on the ground.

The police run over to the demon and I turn around to find Ash. I hear it choke on its own blood and then I hear three shots from the police men's gun. I see Ash and run to him. His face, arms, legs, and stomach are torn and bloody. I put one of my hands on his head and the other on his hand. "Don't worry; we're going to get you to a hospital quick," I say and motion for help to a nearby policeman.

They carry Ash to their car and drive us to the hospital. This is the first time I have ever been out of our small town. It's a poor little town with less than 300 people. Visitors are rare and most people who live here have lived here for generations.

We finally reach the hospital. It's all white and sterile and it smells like chemicals. I look around and see brown leather chairs and a polished marble desk. The policeman who drove us to the hospital walks over to the desk leans in close and whispers to a lady with a blonde ponytail. I see she responds, but I can't hear what they are saying.

The officer backs away from the desk and slams his hands on the desk. "We need to get him in now! Not in thirty minutes!" he yells at her. I see her pickup the phone and speak into the receiver. She forces a smile and speaks so softly, I still can't hear her.

"Okay," he says loudly, and walks back to us. "He can see a doctor in a few minutes," he says before sitting down next to me. Ash is lying on the couch all bloody and his clothes are ripped apart. I feel his forehead; it's hot.

"So are you guys, like, together?" a cop asks me trying to minimize the seriousness of the events we witnessed tonight.

I shake my head no. "Ash is a really good friend, but that's it. I'm pretty sure," I say and look back at him. Ash passed out on the way here and hasn't woken up since.

"Hope he makes it," sighs the policeman.

"He will make it. Ash would not abandon me," I say as I think of my parents. Elle's face flashes into my thoughts. I hope Liam is taking care of her. Why didn't I bring her to the hospital?

Pointing to Ash, the policeman asks, "Where are his parents?

Now I remember why I didn't bring her to the hospital. I don't know if they would take her from me, if they knew we were abandoned. "Liam where are you?"

I must have said his name out loud because I hear the policeman ask, who's Liam?

I sigh. "He's my best friend. I'd do anything for him, except go to the dance." I mumble that last part, and not sure why it mattered anymore.

He puts his hand on my shoulder. "We took care of that masked freak that attacked your friend. Are you going to be okay?" he asks. I'm not sure what to say about what attacked Ash and Elle, but I don't think it was human, so I nod yes.

"Patient Ash Parker," the blonde lady says, checking a clipboard. I raise my hand, and the lady walks over to me and sees Ash still unconscious. She looks at the policeman and asks, "Can you help me get him on the stretcher?" The policeman reaches down and without much effort he lifts Ash onto the stretcher.

We walk down the hall behind the nurse who is pushing the stretcher. The nurse leads us to a room with the numbers 243 in painted gold above the door. As we enter the room a kind-looking man steps into the frame of the door.

"Hello, Audrey. Is this our patient?" he asks her, looking at Ash.

"Yes, Dr. McCray, this is him," she says and she motions to the policeman to assist her. Together they lift Ash from the stretcher and gently place him onto the bed covered in bright white sheets.

The doctor studies Ash carefully, his green eyes moving up and down. He looks like he could be in his late twenties. My eyes trail to his hair, dark blonde with a hint of red. "What happened to him? Was he attacked by a wild animal?" the doctor asks the policeman.

"Something like that." I wasn't sure what to say. If I said he was attacked by a demon creature, he might think I'm crazy.

"Are you from around here?" he asks, not looking at me when he speaks.

"We're all from the same town." I can tell that the doctor had never seen anything like this before. He excuses the nurse, and she walks out of the room. He motions for me to come closer, and I obey his request.

"And where is that?" he asks me.

I notice his breath smells like peppermint. "Pine Hill," I say back to him; wondering if he heard of it.

He looks puzzled. "Where is that?" he asks.

I'm growing tired of his questions. "We have a dying person here! Are you going to fix him or not?" I demand.

He frowns. "Okay, I'll need to remove his clothes to assess the wounds," says the doctor.

"I'm sorry, Miss, but you'll have to leave," the doctor says.

I shake my head. "I'm afraid I can't do that," I respond and take a seat in a hard blue chair.

"I'm afraid you have to leave. Don't worry; your boyfriend will be fine."

I get mad and just blurt out. "He is dying! Help him now!"

The doctor walks over to a machine and presses a button and talks into it. "This is Dr. McCray; I need assistance with the patient and there is an upset girl refusing to leave." Then he turns his attention to Ash and starts to remove his bloody torn shirt.

The same nurse arrives and tells the doctor that assistance is on its way. I'm not sure what that meant, but I wasn't going anywhere. I watch the nurse put a mask on Ash's face, and stick a needle in his arm. She hooked a long tube that was attached to a clear bag hanging from a tall stand. I see the contents of the bag dripping into the tube.

The door opens, and two men garb my arms. They lift me off the ground, and I kick and lash at them until we are back in the lobby. They let me go, and I try to run past them, but they stop me. One of the cops sees me, and threatens to handcuff me to the flagpole outside.

I realize there's nothing I can do for Ash, so I walk outside to get fresh air. I sit down on the grass and start crying. My senses are heightened when I suddenly hear feet walking by me on the sidewalk. My heart starts racing until I look up and see a little girl with dark, silken skin and glasses coming towards me. She sits down next to me.

"Are you ok? Did someone die? Why are you crying?" she asks. I wipe my eyes and look into her lavender-colored eyes.

"How old are you?" I say and push back some stray hair behind her ear.

"I'm eight in one half years old," she says with a smile.

"I have a younger sister named Elle, and you remind me of her. I don't know where she is right now, but I'm sure that she's safe and sound with Liam," I say it out loud for the first time tonight.

"Is Liam your brother?" the little girl asks.

I try to smile and say, "No, sweetheart, he's not. He's my best friend."

Her little girl eyes get really big. "Why are you here?" she asks.

"My friend is not feeling well and the doctors are trying to make him better." I yawn realizing how late it is.

"Harper! Get over here and don't talk to strangers!" a woman calls out to the little girl.

"I have to go," the little girl says with her head down. "I hope your friend gets better." She walks toward where the woman is standing.

"Okay" I call to her. She doesn't turn around but keeps walking until the woman grabs her little hand. I watch them leave and begin crying once more.

I feel a pair of hands touch my shoulders and I spin around to see the policeman standing there. With no expression, he says, "The doctor would like to see you."

We walk back inside and he motions for me to sit

down. I look at the couch that Ash was on; it's now stained red with blood. I slip to the floor and start crying. No one tries to comfort me, and even if someone did, I would push them away. I want Ash back; I need him back. I put my head in my knees and cry some more. I feel a warm hand on my arm and push it away.

"Miss, can I speak with you for a minute?" the doctor's voice rings in my ear. I turn my head, and he helps me to my feet. "About Ash. He is…"

I start crying again. "Dead!" I choke out the words and put my face in my hands. Hearing myself say it out loud makes me cry louder.

"No, he will be fine with some bed rest," he says in a soft voice.

I hug the doctor. "Really? Thank you so much! I thought that he was gone!" I cry.

He smiles. "Do you want to see him? He's awake and asking for you. Only stay for a few minutes, though. He needs to rest."

My mind is racing at the news. I jump up and straighten my wrinkled dress. He isn't dead! He will be better soon! I get to see him! The doctor leads me to Ash's room. The doctor opens the door with the gold 243, and I rush to Ash's side. He smiles when he sees me.

"Finally! A familiar face!" he says, and I start crying again, but this time out of happiness.

I feel his face. "You're really alive!" I squeal and hug him.

"Yep, alive and ready to get out of this place." He looks around, and settles his eyes back on me.

"You'll be out of here soon. The doctor said you need time to heal. So focus on that," I say and smile.

Ash frowns. "I would rather heal at home. Then I can be close to you. Can you stay for awhile?"

I drop my smile and think about this for a second. I want to have as much time with Ash as possible. "I can't stay," I say, and he nods. I glance at the clock. It's three in the morning, and I watch as Ash fights to stay awake. I take his hand in mine; it's cold.

"Don't die on me," I whisper to him.

Ash nods his head. "You know I won't give up, especially when there is so much to lose. We were meant to be together forever" His voice trails off and his hand falls from mine. Ash is asleep.

I watch him for a moment. Studying his features, I whisper back, "As far as you know."

Dr. McCray comes back in the room and forces a smile. "It's time to leave. He needs his rest—you never did say what attacked him."

I swallow hard trying to decide if I should tell the truth. "A demon." I choke out the words.

He walks closer to me and tilts his head as to ponder my response. "It feels like they are all," he tells me. I don't know exactly what that means, but I nod. "It really is sad," he calls to me when I'm about to open the door.

"What is?" I ask him and turn to face him.

He looks at me and says, "Seeing someone you love hurting." The doctor looks back at Ash. I swallow hard.

I take one last look at him and say, "Yes, it is." And walk out the door.

I take the stairs instead of the elevator, but after a few steps, I fall. I don't catch myself; I just slide down the steps one by one. I hit the cold, tile floor and just sit there. My whole body is numb. Everything about me is bruised and battered. I'm tired.

I spot the policeman in the lobby and he walks me to the car. I press my head against the cool glass window and fall asleep.

I wake up in my room and find Elle staring at me, wide-eyed and curious. It's around 4:30 am.

"Serena?" She waves her hand above my face. "Are you awake?"

"Yeah, I'm awake. Did Victoria hurt you?" I grunt and sit up in bed.

"No, she just scared me." She said.

I watch as Elle sits on the side of the bed playing with her messy braid. "Here, turn around," I tell her and I take hold of her hair to fix it. That's when I feel it. Every muscle in my body is aching.

"What happened to Ash?" she whimpers from me tugging on her hair.

"He's at the hospital in Brighton," I tell her. Before she can say anything else, I pull her close to me for a hug. She turns around and hugs me back. I stroke her hair. "You know you mean everything to me. You mean more to me than anyone else, even Ash and Liam," I murmur to her.

"Even our mom and dad?" She tests me.

"Yes, even mom and dad," I confirm.

She lies down in my lap, and I hum a lullaby to her. Her eyes close and she smiles. With my finger, I gently outline her nose, lips, chin, and eyebrows. I used to do this to her when she was younger to help her relax. This technique plus singing was a sure way to put her to sleep. I sing the last words to her from the lullaby. "You are my special someone; you are my everything." I kiss her forehead and shift her little body so we are lying side by side. I continue singing. "Forever and ever," I find myself drifting off to sleep while holding Elle close to me.

I wake up around seven twenty and get Elle up. "Time for school," I urge her. She slowly gets up and walks to her room.

I slide out of my torn dress and slip on a pair of knee-length gray leggings and a gray plaid shirt. I pull on my boots and meet Elle in the kitchen. I don't bother looking in the pantry. We have no food.

I wonder why Aunt Lila hasn't stopped by. Just then I see an envelope on the counter. I recognize it immediately. The envelope is marked in red ink with the words *Girls*. I open it to see money inside. Aunt Lila must have dropped it off when we were out last night. I open the pantry in hopes that she stocked it. I was happy to see she did and we enjoyed some fruit and toast before stuffing our book bags with apples and sandwiches.

We walk in silence until we enter the school; Elle sees two of her friends and tells me good-bye.

On my way to my last class of the day I hear Liam call my name. I turn around and he walks beside me. "Hey, um, so is Ash going to be okay?" he asks with hope in his tone.

I don't know how Liam feels about Ash after last night. "Yes, he will be fine," I tell him.

"That's good news...for you," he snaps sarcastically.

I put my hands on my hips and look at him in disbelief. "Are you serious?" I scream in his face.

"What did I do?" he asks.

"After what happened last night, I thought you

would..." I hesitate before adding, "You know, maybe I do like Ash. Or maybe I don't. That's none of your business, so keep your unwanted sarcasm to yourself," I shout at him.

"So now you like Ash?" Liam spits the words at me. They feel like venom.

"Since when did you care who I like?" I yell at him.

His face turns red, and he yells back, "Since you stopped liking me!" There is a crowd of people gathering now.

"Who says I ever liked you? Who says that I want to be with Ash? Nobody! And I told you we would only be friends, nothing more! So try to wrap that around your big head!" I storm. Liam starts to get really mad at me, but I hold my ground. He wouldn't hit me here. Or would he? Since when does he care what anyone else thinks about him?

He clenches his fist, and I prepare myself for the first blow. But instead, he hits the locker behind me. "Listen!" he screams at me, not taking his hand off of the locker. "You can't like Ash! You don't know anything about him. You just met him!" he yells some more. I can tell there is something else he would like to say, but I spit in his face before he can say another word. I run away as fast as I can, hoping he won't follow.

I speed through the halls, shoving people in the process. I hear Liam pushing his way through the crowd to get to me. I run to the gym and see a baseball bat leaning against the wall. Liam enters the gym, and it's a race to the bat.

I outrun him and scoop it up in my right hand. Liam taunts me. "You won't hurt me! Oh, who am I kidding?

If you had to kill me or Ash, you would pick me in a heartbeat." He smiles and circles me. I keep in sync with his movements, watching every step carefully.

He lunges for me, and I swing the bat hitting the top of his arm. He stops and covers his arm. I look at it too, and I'm a better shot than I thought. I'm distracted by staring at the red mark where the bat struck. He jumps at me and knocks me to the ground. The bat flies across the floor. I try to get up, but Liam is quicker; he pins my arms above my head. I see some boys rush over. They grab Liam and try to pry him off of me, but Liam holds a tight grip. I feel my head pounding.

"Liam!" I scream. "Get off me! You're hurting me!" I feel dizzy and lightheaded. I look into his raging eyes, seeing only emptiness. I'm scared he's turned into someone I don't know. I feel tears streaming down my cheeks and close my eyes. I feel the weight come off me and open my eyes to see Liam running away with the boys chasing him.

"Hey! You feeling okay?" I hear someone say. I nod and notice I'm shaking. He helps me up.

"I feel fine," I tell him and ask if he has seen Liam. He doesn't answer me, but just stares at me.

"Remember me?" he asks. I look at his brown hair, his freckles, and his brown eyes. I'm still shaken and unable to focus.

"Um," is all I can say. I know his face is familiar and before I can speak again he grabs his arm.

"Fifth grade. We were friends until Liam broke my arm for it."

Now I remember. "Oh, yeah, Logan. I'm sorry about that. I didn't want to see you get hurt, so I thought it would be best to…" I break off mid sentence, "Thanks for helping me, even though I didn't deserve it."

He smiles. "You're welcome. I don't think Liam will be bothering you anymore," he says with a chuckle.

I follow him down the hall and he stops in front of the janitor's closet and opens the door. Liam sits inside with his hands tied and his mouth taped shut. Then he sees me and starts saying something that I can't understand. Logan kicks him. I punch Logan in the back, and he falls forward into Liam. He gets up and looks at me. "Consider this payback!" he sneers at Liam.

Logan's friends try to calm me down when I realize what's going on. Without success they take off and leave me in the closet with Liam.

I rip the tape off of Liam's mouth, and look around for something to cut the ropes. "Can you untie me?" he asks. I shake my head no, and he huffs and tries to struggle free.

"Shoot! I don't have my knife!" I yell. Liam smiles and gestures me to look at his back pocket. I do, and I see the top of the blade sticking out.

"Thanks. I really thought I'd lost it for good. If I set you free, are you going to hurt me again?" I ask. He shakes his head no and smiles at me. I grab the knife from his pocket and cut the rope.

He rubs his wrist where the ropes cut into his skin. I reach over and rub his arm where I hit him with the bat. He looks at me. "Since when did you start playing baseball, he chuckles.

"Where did you find my knife?" My fingers wrap around it; the worn out handle feels natural.

"I was at your house when the police brought you

home. I watched you put the knife on the table and so I grabbed it," he explains.

I look at the blade; it has blood on the bottom part of it. I get a flashback of last night events. Liam can see that I'm freaked out and he grabs my hand and leads me outside.

I look up at the sun but only for a second. I blink, and a white dot comes into my vision. "You know you almost killed me," I whisper to Liam.

He sits with his head resting on his knees, and I can see his ears are turning red. "I know," he mumbles.

"You wouldn't kill me, right?" I ask him, but I already know the answer. He slowly lifts his head and looks at me. His eyes are wet and red.

"I don't know; in fact, I don't know anything anymore!" he shouts. I back away, but he grabs my right ankle. I shake it off and sit away from him.

"I'm supposed to be your friend. Why do you lose your temper with me so easily? Sometimes I'm scared of you. I never know what will set you off. Do you get like that with anyone else?" I ask him.

"Like who? Someone like Ash?!" he yells as he hits the ground and gets up to leave.

I get up and walk behind him. I pull out my knife and throw it at his feet. "Just do it now," I tell him. "Just kill me now. But when I'm dead, you're going to regret it!" I see Liam pick up the knife. I'm not sure what he's going to do next. I silently acknowledge the people I'm close to and lower my head.

Good-bye, Elle; thank you for being the best person I've ever known. Good-bye, Liam; thank you for being my best friend for so long. And Good-bye, Ash; thank you for being the closest thing I've ever had to my first love, I think to myself.

Liam approaches me. I picture him positioning the blade to kill me quickly. I know he wouldn't want me to die a painful death. I say a prayer and hope that I will get into heaven. I don't cry. I won't miss this world, because it's been a painful experience since my parents left. I feel his breath in my hair and I squeeze my eyes shut.

"I can't," he says, and I hear the knife drop to the ground.

I open my eyes and see Liam staring at me. I set my hands out in front to block him, but he keeps inching closer to me. I try to push him back, but it's no use. He pulls my head close and kisses me. My head feels like it's spinning, and I feel a warm sensation fill my body. I don't close my eyes; instead, they are wide open.

I push him away and stumble backward, still dizzy and unsure how I feel after he kissed me.

"I'm sorry," he whispers and walks away.

I stand there, not able to move. I watch as Liam walks out of sight. "I'm sorry too," I whisper and pick up the knife.

I'm not sure how much time passed as I walk without knowing where I'm going. I don't notice the fallen tree and I fall into the soft, grassy ground. I stand up and look around; I'm at Ash's river. I think back to the day I met Ash. He's so different from Liam.

I look back at the fallen timber—patches of green moss crawl up the trunk, and the once-green leaves are now a dull brown. I don't recall seeing it there before. I stare at it for a long time. Once a beautiful tree standing tall and now it lies lifeless on the ground.

"Will Ash really be okay?" I wonder aloud. Then I laugh and continue talking to myself. "It's weird how

I live in a world with demons, and the only thing that scares me is that Ash might die." I hear a single gunshot and then I hear twigs snap. I whip around to see what it is. I pull my knife out and wait.

I'm, ready to defend myself in case something tries to attack me. But all I see is a doe and her yearling come into view. The yearling lifts its nose in the air smelling unknown scents. I'm very still and don't want to disturb them. The doe tries to run but it stumbles. It falls to the ground with a bullet hole in its left leg, the yearling stands near her. I run over to it and the yearling runs off into the woods.

A mother deer is dying in front of her yearling.

I start crying, thinking of the abandoned baby deer all alone. It is nearly impossible for me to do it, but the doe is suffering, so I must finish it. I take the knife out cut its throat. I try to stop crying, but I end up sobbing more and more. I wait for the hunter to come for the deer, but time passes and I sit next to its lifeless body and no one comes to claim her. I decide that maybe this was a sign and decided that this doe would feed me and Elle for months.

After I gutted and skinned her, I look for something that I can haul it. I find an old tarp that looks like it once covered a small fishing boat. I lay it out to see if it's durable. I drag it to where the doe is laying and begin to fill the tarp with meat.

Dragging the tarp full of meat is harder than I thought it would be. I stop constantly to rest. On the way back to my house, I think about Liam. If he is really in love with me, then why does he try to hurt me? Should I choose him, Ash, or no one at all? Who would treat me better? I was stupid to even think that; Ash would. If I choose Ash, will Liam still be my friend? Would he go after Ash? If he did, would I be able to live with myself if Liam killed Ash.

I keep to the outside of the Town Square still dragging the tarp behind. I pass three girls who don't pay attention to me because they are laughing and looking at pictures.

Finally, I reach my house. I slowly pull open the door and I drop the tarp of meat. Not from the heavy weight, but from shock.

Our house is completely trashed!

Chairs tipped over, wood floorboards are torn off, books are scattered, and pieces of the small dining table are strewn everywhere. I try to imagine what could have done this. At that moment, the only thing that I can think of that can cause this much destruction are demons.

I hear something smash from Elle's room, and I sprint as fast as I can to her door and look in. A black bear is ripping up everything in her room. I pull my knife from my boot and watch its every move. I see the bear tilt its head back and sniff the air. When the bear catches my scent, he spins around and shows his sharp teeth. I wish that Liam had killed me when I wanted him to; now I'll have to get ripped apart instead and die a slow painful death.

I grip the knife with two hands, waving it at the bear. I had heard somewhere that if you make a lot of noise they may back down and leave you alone. This works when you read about it, but I'm not so sure when you come face to face with it. I chicken out and run to the kitchen trying not to trip over the scattered debris. I hear the bear huffing and growling.

I see my old bow leaning against the wall and grab it. I turn my head to see the bear standing on two legs in the next room. He looks thin and weak for a bear. I wonder if he wondered in the house because he is sick and delirious.

The bear lifts his head and sniffs for a few seconds and then turns to me and growls fiercely, spit flies from his mouth. I grab the arrow and pull the string back. I aim it at the bear's chest and release the string. Apparently my aim was too high. I miss the heart and hit the mouth. The arrow is sticking half-way out its mouth and the bear is thrashing about. I take aim again and this time, I hit my target. The bear falls back and crashes on top of the wooden table.

I watch the bear until I'm sure it's dead. I look around and wonder how I'm going to clean up this mess and get the bear out of the house. Thank goodness Elle is staying at a friend's house tonight. I hate to think what would have happened if she came home and walked in on the bear.

Just then there's a knock at the door. I get up and open the door to see Liam standing there. "I wanted to stop by and…what happened here?" he asks pushing his way into the house. "Where's Elle? Are you okay?" He stops in his tracks when he spots the bear.

"I had a guest" I chuckle

Chapter 4

I tell the man who is selling ice that I will give him the bear hide for five bags of ice. After I describe the color and size of the bear hide, he hands me two bags ice. "I think you'll only be able to take two at a time. When you come back with the bear hide, I'll give you the other three bags." He tells me. I thank him and go home.

I put the ice in the fridge and examine the freshness of the bear meat. I still have to deliver the bear hide and collect the rest of the ice from the iceman before Elle gets home.

I throw the bear hide into a wheelbarrow that belonged to Liam. I was grateful to Liam for bringing the wheelbarrow and helping me clean up the mess caused by the bear. The bear was too heavy for me to move so we worked together to skin it and cut up the meat. Liam was amazingly strong, and we got through it without fighting for once. I offered to give Liam the bear hide, but he suggested I sell it.

The iceman looks very happy when he sees the bear hide. He gives me the last three bags of ice. I rush home and throw the ice in the refrigerator. It's about time for

Elle to come home, so I throw a chunk of the bear meat in a pot to cook. It didn't take long before the meat was tender. I remove the pot from the fire and stab it again with a fork. I taste a small piece and add some salt to help with the flavor. As I reach for the pepper, I hear a knock at the door. I assume it's Elle and unlock the door. Once again, my assumptions are wrong. The door opens and two men, with dark red hair and light blue eyes, grab my arms and lift me off the ground. I scream and kick as hard as I can.

They bring me to the edge of the woods and set me down. One pulls out a black fabric bag and struggles to put me inside it. I scream and squirm and try to get out, but it is tightly secured and I can't tear the fabric. I'm being lifted and thrown over something. I assume it's one of their shoulders, and he starts walking.

"Uh, Harold, I forgot to drug her," the man carrying me says. I hear a thump, and the man carrying me falls backward taking me to the ground with him. I feel a sharp pain in my arm. It feels like I fell on a rock. I try to hold back the tears and concentrate on my escape options.

"Look what you did! You made me drop her!" the man says, picking me up again.

"Whatever. Let's just drug her now," Harold says and unties the bag. I wiggle my arm and hit him in the nose; he stumbles backward and the other guy closes the bag again.

"I can't believe she hit me in the nose. I have something that will take the fight out of her," the other man says and taps something glass. I can't see through the woven bag to figure out what he has planned for me.

"Great! We should have done this earlier. Come on; do it now!" Harold urges him.

"All right. Fine. Be patient" he says. I can feel his hand against the bag trying to hold me down. I squirm more and try to get out of his clutches when I see a tiny needle poke through the bag. I try to get away from it, but it's no use; I feel it prick the top of my leg.

"Ow!" I scream.

"Milo, you got her!" Harold barks, and I feel a cold liquid seep into my leg. As quickly as they punctured my leg with the needle they pulled it out. I reach down and feel where it punctured my skin. I try to find a hole or a dent or something, but there's nothing other than my tender flesh. I start to feel sleepy. They drugged me! I hear the two men talking, but I can't make out what they are saying. I can't keep my eyes open and then blackness.

I'm not sure how long I was out, but when I wake up I feel someone lay me down on a hard surface. I'm still in the sack and I hear people whispering in hushed tones. I'm not sure where I am, so I yell out, "Hey! I'm trapped in this sack thing. Can someone help get me out of it?"

Everyone goes silent, and I hear footsteps coming towards me.

I close my eyes for a second and prepare to fight. As the bag opens, the bright light blinds me at first. When my eyes focus, I see Dr. McCray looking down on me. I waste no time getting out of the bag.

As I look around the room I realize that I'm in the hospital. Someone rescued me from the two creeps. A sense of relief started to form until I spotted the two creeps sitting in a corner staring at me. Panic starts to set in again as I look for an escape route. Dr. McCray must have realized my intentions to run because he grabs my arm. I turn and see the blonde nurse and an older couple standing near the desk. "You woke early," he speaks in a professional voice. I nod at Dr. McCray, not sure what's going on.

"Why am I here? Is Ash okay?" my voice cracks when I utter Ash's name.

"Ash is recovering from his physical injuries," the doctor says. "Our concern now is the state of his mental health. You were the only person that we could ask for help in either finding his parents or provide us information about his mental condition. Ash isn't cooperating with us, so that's why you're here."

I'm confused. "Then why did I get drugged and forced into a bag to be brought here?" I ask him.

He chuckles to himself but quickly stops and looks at me seriously. "Ash keeps talking about demons and that your town is full of supernatural creatures. We were concerned and took precautions to get you here to find out more. We weren't sure if you shared the same mental issues as Ash or if you were a demon, so we used extreme safety measures to get you here. Sorry about that."

When he finishes I look at the two men who kidnapped me. "Do I look like a demon to you?" I say sarcastically.

Dr. McCray extends his hand and raises his dark eyebrows. "We brought you here for information Serena. Can you help us?"

"May I see Ash first?" I ask.

He hesitates for a few seconds and stares at me. "Sure, come this way." He says with a strained smile.

We walk down the hallway to Ash's room. I notice strong odors filling the air. It's a mixture of chemicals and lingering stench from body fluids. I don't know how people can work in a hospital. There are too many sick, injured, and dying people here.

Dr. McCray opens the door, I push pass him and walk towards Ash. I pull up a chair next to Ash's bed and stroke his matted blonde hair. His eyes open, and he smiles. "Hey demon killer." His voice is rough and hushed.

"Hey, how do you feel?" I ask him.

He tilts his head slightly and tries to focus. "I don't know. The doctor gave me some weird pill that makes me tired and numb." He looks at his arm with a needle and tube sticking out.

I try to think of something witty to say back and smile. "That's too bad. I was going to kiss you, but it would be wasted since you wouldn't feel it," I tease him. He tries to laugh, and I laugh with him.

"What does it matter if I can or can't feel it?" he asks me.

I shrug and look away. "Where are those letters you promised you would write me?" I ask, changing the subject.

"I didn't know what to write," he says and looks into my eyes.

"It must be so lonely and boring here," I say.

He nods. "Seriously, were you going to kiss me?" he asks with a hint of hope in his voice. I can't help but smiling. I tilt my head closer to his and slide my hand across his forehead.

"Maybe," I whisper.

I hear someone clear their throat and turn to see Dr. McCray is still in the room. Embarrassed, I motion for him to leave. He mouths the words "I'll be right back" and walks out. I turn back to Ash and notice his face is slightly pink. He must be embarrassed too.

"I didn't know that he was even there," he whispers to me.

"Me either, until a few seconds ago." I smirk.

"I tried to tell them that I need to get out of here. They don't believe me about what happened at the dance. I'm still freaked out about it. I think that's why they keep me medicated, they think I'm crazy. I'm not crazy. Tell me what happened after they brought me here." Ash asks in a desperate tone and trying to whisper.

I bite my bottom lip; that was the one thing I hoped he wouldn't ask. "Do you really want to know?" I mumble.

"Of course," he responds.

I think about telling him everything is fine, but I don't want to lie to him. I take in a deep breath of air and release it. "My house got trashed by a black bear, and Liam kissed me," I say as fast as I can. Ash's eyebrows narrow together and he asks me to repeat what I said. I take in another breath and make eye contact, "My house got trashed by bears, and Liam kissed me."

It takes a second for the information to register. His eyes drop and his forehead wrinkles. He looks defeated when the corners of his mouth drop. "Really?" he moans. I feel bad that I told him. But there's nothing I can do about it.

"I didn't kiss him back, though. I don't think I did anyway." I mumble the last part so that only I can hear it. Ash stares at the ceiling without saying anything. I close my eyes and wonder what Ash is thinking. The first thing that comes to my mind is that he hates me. The second thing is that he hates Liam. I'm lost after that.

I open my eyes, and to see Ash's eyes are closed. I think that's his way of asking me to leave without saying the words. I try to think of something to say but then Dr. McCray comes back in the room. "Your time is up," he says. I bend down and kiss Ash on the forehead; then I walk out with the doctor following me. The hospital seems empty as I look around. Only the two men who brought me to the hospital are standing in a corner whispering to each other.

"Your friend has some wild stories about what goes on in your small town. He said you killed a demon. Can you tell me why Ash would say these things?" Dr. McCray stares at me and I don't answer." "We will need to speak to his parents to see if Ash is taking medication for his condition. Do you know where I can find his parents?" He realizes at this point that I don't have anything to say. "Well then, we will have to deal with this matter without your help." He motions for the men who brought me to the hospital to take me home. I am allowed to ride back to Pine Hill in a car without being put in the sack.

I sit quietly on the ride back. I entertain myself by counting my fingers over and over again until I'm positive that counting fingers is the most boring thing on earth. I play with the tip of my boot until the men who took me stop the car and let me out in front of my home.

I open the door, and run inside. Elle is in the kitchen staring at the clock.

"Elle!" I shout to her. She sees me and runs toward me with her arms open. I pull her into my arms and hug her tightly. "I'm all right. I went to go see Ash," I assure her.

"I know," she tells me. "I found a note under the door that told me where you were, so I wouldn't freak out or tell people you were missing. Then Liam came over and asked where you were. I told him, and he kind of had a melt down or something and started throwing things around. He said some pretty nasty words about Ash that you told me not to say." She lifts up her sleeve to reveal a huge black-and-blue bruise. "The last piece of furniture he threw accidently hit my arm," she says and rolls her sleeve back down.

I grip her shoulders and look straight into her eyes. "Elle, I need you to promise me that you will never listen to Liam when he talks like that," I say. "There's one more thing I need to take care of. Promise you won't follow me." She starts to ask why, but I stop her and make her promise. And when she does, I reach down and grab my knife off the table and stick it in my boot. I see Elle watching me with a concerned face. I run out the door and don't look back.

It begins to rain, and lighting flashes across the sky. I wish I had a jacket to keep me dry. The rain is cold and the winds are getting stronger.

I'm soaked by the time I reach Liam's house. I pound on the door, and he opens it. "Hey, Princess, why are you here?" he asks me. I punch his nose.

"Don't call me Princess!" I yell. "Don't ever come around Elle again!"

His nose starts bleeding heavily. "What is wrong with you?!" he yells back. I slap him across the face, and then run out the door.

"Serena!" he screams. The rain is coming down heavier now and I'm trying to run without looking back to see if Liam is behind me. I can't hear anything except the pouring rain and the splash of water as I run.

The woods aren't very far from his house so I decide to go there for shelter. I spot a tall pine tree and climb it. Once I settled in on a branch high off the ground, I look down to see Liam climbing up the tree. I look up and start to climb higher. I'm careful not to slip. I watch Liam stop climbing and he looks at me. He climbs back down and looks at me from the ground. "Serena!" he screams at me.

I try to climb higher when I see Liam attempt to climb the tree again. This time he climbs almost to where I'm at to show me he can get to me if he wants. He smiles at me and climbs back down to the ground. I grab the branch above my head to steady myself. The branch cracks and breaks off. I lose my footing and fall trying to grab onto a branch to break the fall. I wasn't very successful and felt the hard branches batter me as I fall. I brace myself for a hard impact and wonder if I'm going to end up in the hospital next to Ash. Just then, I landed in Liam's arms. I open my eyes, and Liam is holding me. He glares at me then sets me down.

I look up, and he hits the side of my face. I stumble back and fall over a branch. My cheek feels like it's on fire. I look at Liam's face; his eyes are hard and fixed on my mine. He steps toward me, and I block my face with my arms. Liam grabs my arm and lifts me off the ground. He gently pulls me closer to his body. I'm sickened by how he wants to kiss me again. I turn my head away. Liam takes a hold of my face with both of his hands and turns my face towards him until I feel his warm breath. My heart is still pounding from the fall and I'm trying to slow down my breathing. Without looking away, I put my hands on top of his and remove them from my face. I start to walk away, but Liam grabs my left arm and pulls me close to him again. I try to shake him off, but he holds on tight.

"Serena, please listen." he pleads.

I grab his wrist and try to yank him off. I lean away from Liam and reach in my boot. I pull out my knife and wave it at him. Liam releases me.

"I'm sorry," he says and holds out his hand.

"Your words mean nothing to me anymore," I yell as I slice his out stretched hand. He pulls it back to him and with his good hand knocks the blade out of my hand. I watch it fall. It's stained with his blood. I try to hit him, but he catches my hand and turns it so that I can't move without being in pain. "Liam! Let go!" I scream in his ear. He twists my arm so that it almost snaps and shoves me away.

"Serena, why did you attack me?" he asks in a calm voice.

"Because you hurt my sister! That's why," I yell at him.

He smiles, amused. "Try it. Try to hurt me. You wouldn't stand a chance," he sneers in my face.

I grab onto a tree and pull myself up. "I actually thought that you cared about me. How could I have been so stupid to think that we were friends?" I scream. I feel a lump in my throat start to swell as I shout in his face, "you are a monster! I can't be around you anymore." I sneer at him. "Oh, and by the way, I kissed Ash!"

"What?" he demands.

I stand there facing him, to make sure he hears it loud and clear. "I kissed Ash," I emphasize each word slowly. I expect Liam to retaliate, so I look for any sudden movements from him. Nothing. He just turns away from me and walks the other way. I don't feel bad; I feel like I finally won a battle with him even if it's with words.

I don't know what happened to the little boy and girl who used to agree on everything and do everything together. I guess they grew apart until they became us. Now Liam and I can't even talk to each other without one of us getting hurt. I feel my cheek again; the sting has gone away, but the emotional hurt still lingers. How will I explain the cuts and bruises to Ash? I don't want to lie to him. If I tell him I fell out of a tree, that isn't lying. Of course, he would press me for more details. If I told him the reason I was in the tree, he would go after Liam. I can't let him do that. I think Liam would kill Ash.

My eyes well up with tears and my nose stings. A single salty tear finds its way down my cheek. I wipe the tear away and notice the rain is coming down harder. I can't help but think of Liam and how he must hate me right now. I wander after Liam, afraid he might do something really stupid like hurt himself or someone who crosses his path. My walk breaks into a run, and I call out his name.

"Liam!" I can feel a bruise starting to form on my cheek. I try not to think about what it will look like tomorrow and keep running.

I know him too well; he will ignore my calls and keep going. "Liam, I know you can hear me. I need to talk to you," I holler into the woods. He scares me when he steps out from behind a big oak and leans against it.

"What's there to talk about?" he asks me.

Now that I have his attention, I don't know what

to say, so I just tell him what I think. "We should stop fighting and put who loves who behind us so we can be the friends like we used to be." I can tell that's not what he wants to hear. I don't know why, but I start singing, "Deep in the place where you wait for me, the place with the large oak tree."

He smiles and sings along to a song we made up long ago. "That's the place where we belong, and this is our song." His voice is clear and harmonizes well with mine. He chuckles and looks up at the tree. "Hey, remember when I used to kick your butt in acorn wars?"

I give him a dirty look. "I remember it the other way around," I taunt him.

He picks up an acorn and throws it at me. "This means—," and at the same time we scream, "War!" We each get behind a tree and start picking up acorns off the ground. I store mine next to me, but as soon as Liam gets one, he throws it at me. When he goes to gather more, I pelt him with a handful of acorns. He guards his face with his arms, but I'm too good an aim and hit the top of his head. He holds his hand up.

"Truce, truce!" he yells.

"Nope, I'm having too much fun!" I yell back with a smile and hit him with more acorns. When he has collected enough acorns, he heads back to his tree. He doesn't throw any, and I get suspicious. I slowly walk over to his tree and look around the trunk. He's gone. I huff and think to myself that he couldn't deal with the fact that I'm the acorn champion. I turn to head back to my tree when Liam pops out from another nearby tree.

"Ah!" he screams and starts hitting me with acorns. I block my face.

"No fair! Ambush attack!" I shriek.

"All is fair in love and war!" he says back and bends down to gather some more acorns. I pick them up faster and chuck them at him. He laughs, and then so do I.

I didn't realize it, but when we were destroying each other with the acorns, the rain started to let up. The sun begins to peak over some dark clouds. "This was fun," I say and turn away from him.

Liam catches my arm and turns me around. "We have more to catch up on," he smiles. We run to the small pond nearby and jump in. The cold water soothes my wounds, and I go under the water until I can't hold my breath any longer. I take in a huge gulp of air and go back under the water again. I come up for air again and see Liam standing at the edge of the pond. I start to go under again and stop when I see him backing up.

"What are you doing?" I ask him. He runs forward and jumps in the water, splashing me. He comes up, and I splash him back. We start a splashing contest. Liam ends up winning that one.

We get done playing around in the water and wring out our dripping clothes. I lie back on the soft grass and look up at the sky. "Just like the old days," I whisper.

Liam lies next to me. "Not quite; you didn't know that I liked you in the old days," he mumbles in my ear. I start to turn over to warm my back side when I see a shadow of a figure. I look up to see Ash standing there. He looks healthy again with some minor cuts and bruises still showing; his blonde hair is moving slightly in the wind, and he's looking at me smiling.

I fumble over my feet to get to him. I throw my arms around him, and he catches me before I stumble over my own feet. "Why are you out of the hospital?" I quietly say into his ear. I hear him laugh a bit.

"They said I was well enough to leave, and I stopped talking about the demons. So they let me out of that prison," he whispers into my hair. I feel strange with Ash and Liam in the same place after what I told them both. I remember my exact words to Ash. *"My house got trashed by bears, and Liam kissed me."* I think back to what I said to Liam. *"And I kissed Ash!"* My voice rings in my head. Ash still holds onto me, and I slowly pull away from him. "Well, it's great to have you back," I say without making eye contact with either of them.

"So did you two kiss some more when I was gone?" Ash raises his eyebrows at me and then Liam. I feel my face burning from embarrassment.

"No," I assure him. But right when he starts to believe me, Liam has to barge in.

"Yes, yes we did," he smirks at Ash. I bury my face in my hands and shake my head.

"Really? Because I believe her!" Ash sneers at him. I knew this would happen.

"Yes we did, under a pine tree that she fell out of." There is a pause, and knowing Liam, he is saying this to irritate Ash. "And I caught her when she fell! Bet you can't catch her in *your* condition!" he snarls at Ash looking at the scratches and giant bruises covering his arms, neck, and some of his face.

I take my hands away from my face. Ash is looking at me to confirm or deny it. I look away from Ash and face Liam. "No we didn't! Remember, you tried to, but we didn't kiss!" I scream at Liam. He and Ash turn their heads in my direction.

Ash points at me and smiles. "So you didn't kiss!" he hisses at Liam. Liam squints at me, and I can tell he is mad that his plan didn't work.

"The only reason he caught me is because he felt bad when he drove me up the tree," I mutter under my breath. Liam grips my arm, and Ash looks at him with cold, mean eyes.

He gets close to Liam's face and shoves his finger into his chest. "If you ever touch her, I will—" He doesn't finish, because Liam laughs at him.

"You'll what? You wouldn't stand a chance against me!" Liam yells as he shoves Ash back.

I gather enough courage to take a hit from Liam and get in between them. Liam pushes me away. I stumble and Ash catches me before I fall. I get a great idea and take my knife out. Ash and Liam are already getting in each other's faces. I get as close to them as I can and scream as loud as I could. They stop bickering for a second and look at me. I raise my knife to my throat.

"Liam, if *you* hurt Ash, this will be going through my neck. And, Ash, if *you* hurt Liam, this will go through my neck. Got it?" I scream at them.

"You wouldn't slice your neck," Liam says and pushes Ash over. I take the blade and press it against my skin; I slowly tear my flesh about an inch and stop. I feel pain, but I want to make a point. I hope Liam doesn't call my bluff.

"Want to bet?" I ask, putting my hand underneath my neck. Blood drips on it; I look at Liam and smirk. His expression goes numb, and his face turns pale white. Ash rushes to my side and holds my neck.

"Don't worry about it," I tell him. "I want to bleed to

death so Liam can understand that I am *dead* serious!" I say the last part with a smile. Ash just puts more pressure on my throat. "Oh, even better! Ash, put more pressure on my throat. You can choke me to death instead!" He releases my neck, and the blood is stopping.

Liam just stands there, frozen and pale. I think I made my point and walk away. Ash comes after me and touches my arm. I jump. "Serena, what was that about?" he asks. I start to cry and he wraps his arms around me and pulls me close to him. The moment feels right, so I lean my head on his shoulder.

As we walk through town on our way to my house, I notice the townspeople ignoring us. No one smiles or says hi to us; they just look away and keep walking. We arrive at my house and I ask Ash if he wants to stay for awhile, but he declines and I kiss his nose. He smiles and walks away.

"Good night!" I say and wave as he walks away. He turns before he is out of sight and waves back.

Elle is sleeping on the couch covered in blankets. I go over to her and pull them up to her chin. I kiss her forehead and sleep next to her on the floor.

CHAPTER 5

Daylight seeps in through the window and brushes my eyelids. I wake up and lay there listening to Elle breathe. I get up to go make breakfast using the bear meat. I open the fridge; a quarter of the ice has melted. I take out the meat and put it in a pan to fry. Next, I spread butter on 4 slices of bread and fry it for a minute until it's toasted. After the meat is brown and tender I put it in between two slices of bread.

Elle comes into the kitchen and sits down at the table. I put a plate in front of her with the sandwich still steaming and kiss the top of her head. I sit down and watch Elle eat. We are both silent eating our bear breakfast. I think about what happened last night and wonder if Liam made it out of the woods? Should I check on him or assume he found his way back home? Guilt starts to set in and I decide I need to know if he is okay. We finish eating breakfast and I ask Elle to clean up the kitchen because I need to run out for a few minutes.

I head out into the woods to find Liam. Even though my stomach is full from breakfast; it's churning from worry. I grab my waist and notice I've lost a few pounds since my troubles with Liam and Ash started. I try to find the spot where Liam passed out last night. Without much search effort I find him lying on the ground; his black hair is covered in mud, his body is slightly exposed from his torn clothes. At second glance I can see blood stains on the shredded clothes still left dangling from his body. I drop down on my knees next to him. I quickly remove my shirt to cover him up. The morning air is chilly on my bare arms wearing only my sleeveless gray shirt. I gently tap his face.

"Liam, Liam, wake up!" I beg him. His eyes flutter a bit, and I start crying either because I'm so happy he isn't dead or because of the guilt I feel for leaving him there. I can't tell which. I start to panic and start screaming, "Help! Someone! Anyone! Help!" No one comes. I lift his head off the ground and set it in my lap. "Oh my God! Who did this to you? Or…what did this to you?" I ask him. But he is too weak to speak. I try to call for help again, but this time I stand up so my voice will carry. "Help! Please help me! I need someone! Please!" I scream. I kneel down beside him again and begin sobbing harder.

"It's going to be okay," I keep telling him. "Someone is going to find us." I repeat these words over and over trying to convince us both that someone will help us. I lightly brush the dirt off of his face as best I can. His skin is so beautiful. I hear cracking branches from a distance and pray it's someone and not something in the woods. Hope creeps inside me as the sound of cracking branches grows louder. "Over here! Help!" I cry. I try to force a smile and hold back the tears before I look into Liam's eyes and try to give him hope. "It's going to be all right, I promise you."

I take his hand in mine; it's cold with scratches and cuts. I look him over to see blood seeping from a wound in his lower leg. I hear someone calling out in the near distance, and I turn in that direction. I see a man, come into sight and he look towards us. "Please help my friend!" I beg. As he draws nearer he looks to be around eighteen or nineteen. He sees Liam and pulls out a water container strapped to his belt. He begins splashing cold water onto Liam's cuts, washing away the blood and dirt. I'm truly grateful for his help, but I'm not sure if he can be trusted. I don't know why I think that since I don't know him; I guess I don't have a choice at this moment but to trust this stranger to help Liam.

He pours the last of the water on Liam's face and looks at me. "What happened to your friend?" he asks. I look at Liam's arms and legs, and shrug. I hug my chest and start rubbing my chilled arms. "I think he needs to see a doctor for those cuts. He may get an infection if he doesn't get treatment." He turns back to Liam and studies his injuries. He stands up and says, "The wounds don't seem to be too deep and it doesn't appear he has any broken bones. He may have a slight concussion and that's why he is dazed. There's not much I can do for him. Make sure your friend sees a doctor." He repeats. "I'm late and need to go." He starts to leave and I stand up to face him.

"Well thanks for your help. You can carry on with whatever you were doing," I say through my teeth.

He senses that I'm tense and puts his hand on my shoulder. "Your friend will be fine," he calmly tells me.

I brush his hand off of my shoulder. "Thanks again for the help," I say, irritated.

I watch his eyes look me over from head to toe. "I can't remember what you said your name was," he says.

"That's because I didn't tell you my name. I don't think we will be seeing each other again." I say, hoping he would leave so I could attend to Liam.

He shrugs. "Maybe," he winks.

I roll my eyes. "Goodbye!" I utter and turn away from him. He walks into the woods without another word. I turn my attention to Liam. Liam is more aware and trying to sit up.

"Liam, what happened to you?" I demand.

His eyes look down his damaged body. "I'm not sure. It was sort of a dog-type animal that attacked me. Maybe it was a coyote." His voice is muffled and low.

"Maybe it was a wolf," I mumble under my breath. Now that I think about it, some people from town reported seeing a wolf near town a few months ago. Liam said it was a dog thing, but he wasn't sure. But why would a wolf attack Liam? I think back to the wolf that attacked Elle. That wolf was sickly and Elle is small and he may have mistaken her for small prey. Besides, I killed that wolf. Nothing can live after getting speared through the stomach. There must be a pack of them living in the woods. "What color was it?" I ask him.

"Dark brown," he replies, wincing in pain.

"I'm going to carry you back to my house, okay? Well, maybe drag you." I say, laughing a little. He flinches when he tries to laugh at my rescue plans.

I feel awkward sliding my hands under his back and neck to help him to his feet. He strains as he stretches his leg and puts pressure on it. I look around and see a thick branch near a tree. I grab the branch, and rip off the sleeve from my shirt that covered Liam. I tie the branch to his leg with the torn sleeve to help keep his leg straight. He lets out a faint scream from the pain.

I find another large branch and give it to him to use as a cane to help take the pressure off his leg. As we start to walk or limp in Liam's case, I look down and see the wound on his leg start to bleed again. I stop and put my hand over it and apply pressure to get it to stop. After a few minutes, I pull my hand away to examine his wound and when I saw all the blood on my hand, I lost it. I run over to a bush and vomit.

I walk back over to him, and rub my bloody hand down his shirt. My hand felt sticky even though most of the blood was gone. I don't think Liam cared that I stained his frayed shirt. I weave my arm around his arm, and support his weight. At first his weight wasn't too strenuous, but after about twenty minutes of walking it was taking a toll on both of us. We stop for a few minutes to rest. He starts to tell me something, but then goes quiet. Then we continue until we reach my house.

I set him down when I make it back inside the house. Elle sees us and freezes in place. I don't have time to explain what happened to Elle but ask her to ask a neighbor for some ointment. She leaves immediately and I get to work on Liam. I take a wet cloth and carefully wash his cuts. I take his shirt off last, because I feel uncomfortable. He has so many cuts that I can't count them all.

By the time I wipe off the remaining blood Elle is back and hands me a tube of ointment. I put some ointment on his gashes. I use most of it up. I pray this is enough to ward off infections.

He is asleep by the time I'm finished. I leave his shirt

on the ground, since it was such a chore to get it off and it was ripped and stained. His hair is covered in leaves, small twigs, and dirt.

I start removing them from his hair and notice his skin is very hot. I feel his forehead with the back of my hand; it's burning up. I know that's a sign of a fever which may be caused from an infection.

"Elle, take care of him please. Get him anything he needs," I yell to her, and she nods. I open the door and walk out. As soon as I'm outside, an adrenaline rush kicks in and I try to figure out what to do next. It's a crazy idea to think Ash will help Liam, but I don't have another option. I run until I reach a small red-and-brown wooden house. I knock on the door, and a very beautiful woman with blonde hair and green eyes opens it slowly.

"Hello, who might you be?" she asks.

"Hi, I'm here for Ash," I tell her.

She shifts her hands onto her hips. "You must be Serena. It's nice to finally meet you. I'm his mother. Ash just left to find you." She smiles. She has the same smile as Ash.

"Did he say where he was going?" I ask, breathing heavy.

"He didn't say exactly, but I suppose he would start by going to your home first. If you didn't pass him on the way, he may have cut through the woods. Is there a problem?" She frowns.

"No, no problem at all," I tell her.

Her smile returns to her face, and she thanks me for stopping by. I dash off to the woods and see Ash through the trees. I'm a few yards behind him when I scream his name. He turns around. I feel for my knife in my boot and take it out. Ash looks at me like I'm crazy. I wave the blade in the air. "Come and get me! You attacked Liam, now it's my turn. Come and get me!" I yell at the woods.

"What are you doing? What happened to Liam?" Ash asks me. I just push him behind me.

"Watch my back," I demand.

"Huh?" He says, obviously confused.

"Cover my back!" I scream. Ash stands behind me with our backs only inches apart. "Take out your knife," I say with authority.

"How did you know that I had one?" he whispers.

"I know everything," I tell him. Actually, I saw the top of it in his boot when I cut my neck. He pulls it out; it's longer than I expected. The knife is about eight inches long with jagged edges and a hooked tip. It's nothing like I've ever seen before. My knife is a simple smooth blade about six inches long. I wonder if Ash ever killed an animal with a knife before.

Silence.

I take this moment to turn around and hug Ash, knowing that this might be our last moment together. He hugs me back and accidently drops his knife. I see it on the ground and bend down to pick it up. Halfway down I see a creature; half wolf, half human thing charge toward me and Ash. He doesn't see it, because he is still turned around. I grab the handle and hold it with confidence. "When I say jump, jump to your left," I yell to him.

"Okay," he says. I wait until the thing is about eight feet away and scream for him to jump. He jumps right on time and leaps away to safety. The animal leaps at me, and I manage to stab it in the gut and watch it fall in front of me. When it gets up, blood trickles down its fur, staining the chestnut-colored coat. It looks at me and growls. It turns its head toward Ash and starts to slink towards him. I run to Ash and push him back on the ground and guard him with my body. The blood from Ash's knife is dripping onto my hand.

The animal launches forward and swats me with its paw, knocking me to the ground. The claws are sharp, and they rip into my hip. I feel a sharp pain and see the blood soaking my pants. I look up to see the animal stalking Ash.

I jump back to my feet and sprint towards Ash. It springs in the air and lands on top of Ash, tearing at him with razor-sharp claws and teeth. I jump on the animal's back and dig both of the blades into its sides. It yelps in pain and starts thrashing from side to side trying to do away with the blades stuck inside it. I watch the animal lay on its side and try to use the ground to knock the one blade out. I use this opportunity to jump on its back and grab the handles and slide the knives deeper into its body.

The beast shakes violently and tries to bite me. I fall to the ground trying to avoid its teeth and claws. I roll onto my back and look up to find it standing over me and staring down at me with its teeth showing. I look into its brown eyes and notice they are the same color as mine. One of the blades falls from its back, and I quickly grab it. The animal stands over me with its legs on either side of me. I shove the knife into its chest. It lunges at me, but it falls onto its side. I move away before it clamps down on me. It lifts its head up and then it stands up and hobbles over to me and falls again.

I run over to Ash and see his shirt sleeves are torn to shreds where he protected himself. He assures me it's not serious and holds out his hand to me. I take it and hold it against my heart.

"Do you feel that? That is my heart beat. It beats for you Ash. You're a part of my life and I don't want to lose you." I cry and continue to hold his hand to my chest. I hear the animal wince from behind me and turn around.

The animal is gone but a man with dark brown hair and eyes lays there where the animal fell to the ground. I run over to where he is struggling to sit up. Before the words come out of my mouth, I recognize him instantly. He has the same brown eyes and thick dark hair, as someone I know and love so much. There was no mistaking his square jaw and dimpled chin. But how is it possible?

"Dad?" I say with a lump in my throat.

He grabs my hand and pulls me down to where he sits so we are facing each other. He kisses my forehead. "Serena. My little fighter. You're so grown up," he says and kisses my hand. I can tell he is fighting to stay alive, but I have so many questions to ask him before he leaves me again.

I start firing off questions without thinking. "Why are you here now? What just happened? Where is the injured animal that attacked me and Ash? Why did you abandon us?" I start crying and pounding on his chest.

His hands are shaking as he grabs both my hands to stop me from hitting him again. I look at him as if he will disappear any second. I watch the color vanish from his face. "I left because I didn't want to hurt you," he says. "It was difficult decision for me to leave you and Elle alone, but I didn't have a choice. I have the werewolf gene." He starts to choke up as he finishes explaining.

"Where's Mom?" I ask, wiping my eyes. His eyes start to shut. "Dad, where is she?" I ask again.

"You're mother inherited the gene just like I did. She had two other sisters who were lucky and are human. We thought we were lucky to so we got married and—" he pauses, "when we were in our late twenties and didn't transform, we thought we didn't inherit the gene either so we decided to have children. One day, your mother transformed and we were devastated. She had no choice and left. I stayed behind to take care of you and your sister. It wasn't long after that and I showed signs of transforming. I asked your aunt Lila to look after you because I knew I would have to leave you to. I know what you're going through Serena. Our parents left us when we were young. It's not easy growing up without parents. Your mom and I were best friends growing up, just like you and Liam. When we left, we knew one day—how do I put this? Um, you would have to—"

I interrupt him. "No, please no," I beg him.

"You have to if you have the gene," he protests.

"I don't have *the* gene," I say.

He shakes his head. "No, you don't understand. You have strength and instincts that come from being a werewolf. It will happen one day and when you transform, you will need to be with someone who understands that life. If you don't marry Liam, you will be alone," he pleads.

"I don't care if I'm alone," I tell him.

"You have to," he whispers and fades away before he can finish telling me what happened to our mother.

I turn to see Ash staring at me and then at the man laying dead next me. "That was my father the werewolf," I say. Ash walks over and pulls his knife out of my father's side. He reaches under my father's leg and recovers my knife and hands it to me.

We walk towards my house in silence. On the way, I try to process everything my father said. It finally hits me; that's why Liam gets violent when he's angry. It must be a werewolf thing. I try to blink away the tears that start to flow.

How can this be happening to me? I just poured my heart out to Ash and now I can't be with him. Even if I choose not to be with Liam, I can never be with Ash. Is this what Liam has been hinting at these last few days. He already knows what we are to become?

I start to wonder if my father was watching out for me this whole time. Did he see I was falling in love with Ash and he tried to kill him because I couldn't be with Ash? But why would my father attack Liam? Did Liam try to stop my father from going after Ash? Was Liam on his way to warn me, and my father made sure he wouldn't? My father probably reasoned that if Ash was out of the picture, Liam wouldn't have any competition.

I think about my parents and wonder if they had a relationship like me and Liam. Would I be happy if I married Liam?

Ash and I walk through the door and Elle runs up to me and wraps her arms tightly around my waist. She looks up at me and says, "I thought I'd never see you again. Liam told me you were being foolish and putting yourself in danger for reasons you don't understand."

I look at Liam, wide-awake and alert. He sits on the

couch looking smug. "Hey, Princess, you made it home alive and saved your almost boyfriend! Good for you!" He claps his hands. I can't believe I'm hearing this from him. Liam knows that I figured out what's really going on.

"You knew all this time and didn't say anything? You put us all in danger and didn't say anything! You've been hesitating to tell me something for days. Is this what you were keeping to yourself? Why Liam?" I say. I have no fight left in me and it shows on my face.

"Why what?" he smirks. "Why didn't I come clean when I found out I was different? At first, I thought it was just me, but then I saw how tough and spirited you are and knew that it was in your blood also. You could say I sensed it." He smiles and signals me to come closer. I lean in close, and he whispers into my ear, "Did you know that we are meant to—"

I close my eyes and back up. "I know, I know! My father told me before he died. But there's still a chance I'm not like you." I tell him with confidence.

He shakes his head. "You're in denial. You're just like me." He moves closer to me. I break eye contact and look down and notice the gashes and cuts on his arms are almost gone.

"H-h-how did you recover so fast?" I stutter.

"Werewolf blood," he smiles.

"Wait, I don't understand." I utter. "Why did my father die and not recover from the wounds? Is my father really dead?"

He nods and smirks at Ash. "He never stood a chance."

Reality sets in and my eyes glaze over with tears. "I killed my own father!" I cry. I hear a glass shatter and turn around to see Elle standing there with broken glass at her feet. With all the commotion, I forgot she was in the room. Elle stares at me horrified to learn that I killed our father. "Elle, I'm sorry you had to find out like this. I need to explain everything that happened today."

My attention is drawn to Liam when he pipes up and says, "Yes, I guess you did kill daddy! But you didn't do it alone!" he looks at Ash standing there holding his knife.

I look at Liam and point my finger, "Shut up Liam! I should kill you right now for bringing Elle and Ash into this!" I say disgusted.

"Sorry Elle. Big sister just found out that she's going to be a werewolf one day and three's a crowd...right *ash*tray?" he goads me.

I can't hold back the anger any longer; I slap Liam's face as hard as I can. "I refuse to be with you, EVER!" I say shaking my hand to ease the sting.

"Well you can't be with Ash either. You know what will happen once you transform, he'd be dog food...or should I say werewolf chow," he shouts back.

Liam leaps across the room and grabs Ash by the throat. "I could make this easy for you Serena. I know if you kill lover boy, you couldn't live with yourself. However, if I kill him, you would owe me...if you know what I mean." He smiles wide and raises his eye brows.

I see the fear in Ash's face. "Get away from him!" I scream at Liam.

Liam gets real close to Ash's face and snarls. "Today is your lucky day ashtray. I want to tattoo this moment into your memory permanently so if you get the urge to be with Serena this will deter you." Liam quickly picks up a piece of broken glass and carves the letter S in Ash's arm. I watch as Ash struggles to get away from Liam. I lunge for Liam and tackle him to the ground and away from Ash.

Ash grabs Elle and they move to the other side of the room. Liam tries to shove me off, but I stay put. I hold his shirt and punch him in the nose. I watch blood stream from his nose.

Liam manages to push me off and scurries across the room to grab my knife. I try to get to the knife before Liam, but he reaches it before I do and runs to where Ash and Elle are standing. Elle jumps in front of Ash and with one swipe of his arm Liam hurls Elle out of his way. She falls against what is left of the dining table. I run over to Elle and she tells me she's not hurt. I tell her to run and hide somewhere. She does as I say and runs into her room.

Liam holds the blade to Ash's neck. "I think you're luck just ran out," he grins at Ash. I reach down and pickup a large piece of jagged glass and lodge the sharp edge deep into the middle of his back. He spins around to face me and reaches back to remove it. I grab Ash's hand and we run for the door. On the way, Ash hands me his knife. I look back to see Liam pull the glass object from his back. He doesn't wince and holds it up like a trophy for me to see. "You have to kill me to stop me," he smirks.

I grip the knife with my right hand and wave it at him. "That can be arranged," I shout back. I see Elle peeking out her door watching us. "Elle, go!" I command her.

"Stay! Watch me destroy your sister's boyfriend!" Liam screams at her. She bursts into tears and slams the door shut behind her.

Liam growls and his eyes change to a silvery blue color. I stop in my tracks unable to move as my body starts to shake uncontrollably. My vision is blurry and I close my eyes to adjust. When I open them, everything I see is detailed and sharp. My senses are heightened and I hear the slightest sounds all around me. I see Ash watching me in horror, but I can't speak. "I think today is my lucky day," Liam sneers. I want to say something to Ash, but nothing comes out of my mouth. I touch my lips and they feel bigger than usual. I rub my fingers across my teeth and panic sets in when I feel the sharp daggers. I look at Liam in disbelief and watch as his teeth start to grow into sharp points.

I pull my hands away from my mouth and see my fingernails grow into razor-sharp claws; I grip my hands in pain. My skin feels like it is crawling. When I go to scratch my arm, I see large amounts of hair growing rapidly. This can't be. I look down to see my feet bust through my shoes and my once petite feet are now hairy paws with long nails. My chest feels tight and my clothes shred off me as my figure changes. I release a low growl. My thoughts are jumbled and I try to focus on my next move. I see Liam has transformed into a werewolf and is starting to pace. I feel the urge to protect my territory and assume position on all fours; it feels natural. I turn my head to see Ash's eyes widen, and he passes out. Liam is still a bit bigger than I am, and I worry a little. He has one goal—kill Ash. I also have one—kill Liam.

He charges me. I charge back, and we end up knocking heads. Liam has no interest in killing me; he just wants Ash. He swats at me, and I sink my teeth into his paw. I pounce on him and try to bite his neck, but he claws my face. I bite into his head until I hear a cracking sound. I let it go, and Liam backs up, pawing at his bleeding ears and skull. He bears his teeth at me, and I do the same back. My new legs are fast, super fast. I run after him, wrestling him, snapping my powerful jaws. I strike him a few times with my paw in the face and chest.

Liam retreats further back and starts to change back to his human form. He holds his hand up gesturing for me to stop attacking him. I see he's breathing hard and I back up a few steps.

Exasperated, Liam pleads, "Serena, I'll make you an offer you can't refuse. If you agree to marry me, I won't harm Ash. If you don't agree, then you leave me no choice but to kill him. Think about our future—you and me, in the woods together, *alone*." Elle's face turns a ghostly pale. I snort at him. "Don't you understand, we were meant to be together."

"Liam, you're the one who doesn't understand. You're not giving me a choice." I show my teeth to Liam and growl.

He narrows his eyes and shakes his head as he's trying to quickly transform back into his werewolf form. His voice is unrecognizable as he stares at Ash. "Sorry ashtray. It looks like this is the end of the line for you." His eyes start to change colors and I take this opportunity to leap on top of him with my jaws wide open. Liam is trapped under me and my mouth encloses around his head. I hesitate for a second before biting down. I shake his head violently until I don't feel any movement. I can taste blood as it fills my mouth.

I let go and his head falls to the ground. I change back into human form and look down at Liam's lifeless body. I feel horrible for killing my long time friend, but I'm not going to be with someone if I don't love them. I stand there staring at Liam lying on the floor motionless. Both bad and good memories of our time together start to fill my head. I'm not sure how much time passed when I glance at Ash standing there with a frightened look. He's stares at me as if I'm going to pounce on him.

I smile a fake smile and shout to the heavens, "Thanks mom and dad! You made me kill my best friend. Is that the kind of life you wanted for me? What's next?" Purging my feelings into the empty air didn't make me feel any better. I look back at Ash again and realize he must be thinking he's next. I gag as I feel blood in the back of my throat. I spit until the last of the blood in my mouth is gone.

"Ash. Ash, it's over." I shake his shoulders. He opens his eyes and pulls my head to his face and kisses me for a long-lasting time. I hear the bedroom door open and see Elle look out. I pull away from Ash and run to her. Elle's face is red and wet from crying and she falls into my open arms. I look over at Liam's body and hope this is the end of it.

Ash walks over to where we are and pulls us all together in a group hug and whispers in my ear. "Thank you for saving my life. I'm still trying to process everything that happened."

"I couldn't let Liam kill you. I...I...care about you too much and I'm still trying to process that," I say and throw my arms around him. He smiles and kisses my cheek. "So do you think Elle is a...?" he stops himself before saying werewolf.

I shrug. "I hope not. The gene isn't always passed

down to the next generation. She may have a chance to be normal, at least according to what my father told me," I say to him.

"Are you going to be ok Serena?" Ash looks concerned. I nod. "So where do we go from here?" he inquires.

"I'm not sure," I tell him. He pulls me into a hug. "I'm new to all this and I'm not sure how it works."

"We can get through this," he assures me.

"I hope so." Elle looks up at both of us and pats our backs.

He pulls me and Elle closer to him. Elle pushes away. "This is too mushy for me," she says and walks away. We watch her leave and shut the door to her room. We smile at each other and Ash grabs me by the waste and picks me up and starts spinning me around in circles.

CHAPTER 6

Two weeks later ...
I wake up, fully rested and wide-awake. I get up and shut my bedroom door to get dressed. I take off my pajamas and slide on a red sweater and a pair of dark jeans. I grab a pair of socks and walk to the kitchen to start making breakfast.

It's the middle of fall, and the temperatures have been staying below normal. Elle's nightmares are starting to diminish. It's been five days since she woke me up screaming in the middle of the night. I'm happy to report that my nightmares are also going away. Ash spends most of his time here with me and Elle; he calls Elle his little sister. It's nice to have him around.

I'm starving and look to see what we have to eat. I take out some eggs provided by Ash's mother and the milk. I smell the milk to make sure it's still fresh and decide it is and set it on the table next to a ceramic bow. I crack 4 eggs against the side of the bowl and start to beat the eggs. I stop in my tracks and don't move when I hear a strange noise coming from the living room. I grasp the fork in my hand tightly and walk quietly towards the noise. Elle and Ash jump out from behind the couch and yell happy birthday. I drop the fork that I'm carrying and hold my heart. "You guys nearly gave me a heart attack!" I shriek, and they laugh and high five each other.

"Happy birthday, Serena!" They both say in harmony.

"We got you something," Ash says as he hands me a small box. Elle follows him and hands me a bigger box.

"You're going to love it!" she squeals and smiles at Ash.

I honestly forgot it was my birthday today. I put the small box down and lift the lid to the larger box to find a brand new bow with a sheath and five arrows inside. A flashback of the bear attack comes to mind and I quickly erase it and smile at Elle. "You're right. I do love it. Thank you so much!" I say and hug Elle.

Ash picks up the small box and hands it to me. "Happy birthday," he whispers into my hair. "I hope you like it," he says, pushing my hair out of my eyes. Without even opening it, I know what it is. I open it slowly trying to savor every second. My mouth drops open when I see a shiny silver ring with a small blue sapphire sparkling in the light. I lower my eyes from the ring to see Ash bending down on one knee. "Serena Coleman, will you…"

Before he can finish, I crouch down and hug him. "Yes! Yes! A million times yes!" I say.

"She said yes Elle!" I see him choking on his words as he looks into my eyes, "I wasn't sure you would say yes."

"Are you sure you can be with me, knowing what you know? I ask.

"Yeah, it's crazy. Right?" he says with a half smile.

"No, it's love!" I say and kiss his cheek. Elle walks away.

"I'll be in another room until breakfast is ready," she calls and walks out.

"We need to wait a few years before we do this," I whisper to him. With that, he slides the ring onto my finger.

I hold out my hand and admire how beautiful it looks on my finger. I grab his arm. "After breakfast, we need to tell your parents our plans," I smile. Don't you agree?" I ask.

"Fine," he says, as I rest my head on his shoulder.

PART TWO

CHAPTER 7

I t has been a while, and I haven't shown any signs of transforming into a werewolf since that horrible day with Liam. I've concluded that if I can control my temper, I can stay human.

Life has been uneventful for Ash, Elle and me since Liam died. Ash keeps busy with hunting and giving swim lessons to young kids. Elle prefers to hang out with us and fish at the pond after school. She refuses to go hunting with me and Ash. I'm sure she's seen enough bloodshed to last her a lifetime. I don't push her to hunt.

Ash's mom, Mrs. Parker, has grown fond of her. Elle goes to Ash's house twice a week and collects chicken eggs for the Parkers. They let Elle take some eggs home with her. I'm staying busy with school, taking care of Elle and trying to plan our future. The three of us spend a lot of time together. I suppose the secret we share bonds us. I think about this as I lie in my bed staring at the ceiling.

I pull the blanket off and sluggishly crawl out of bed. It's chilly outside the covers, so I put on a heavy shirt over my t-shirt.

Aunt Lila hasn't been by the house in a long time

and I'm beginning to grow worried. She has always been there for us more or less, but since my father died she hasn't come by the house. I wonder if she knows. Maybe she's afraid that one day she will stop by and find herself coming face to face with a werewolf. I'm sure she knows there's a possibility that I could turn out to be just like my parents.

I put on two pairs of socks and head to Elle's room. I knock on her door. "Elle, you up?" I whisper through the door.

"Yeah," she replies sleepily. She obviously remembered our plans to go walking this morning or she would still be sleeping.

"Are you dressed?" I ask, putting on my jacket and boots.

"Almost," she says and steps out a minute later. She is wearing the cutest yellow hat with a heavy coat, a pair of jeans, and at least two pairs of socks. I don't blame her either; it's cold during the winter season. My jacket is a heavy red one, and my boots are starting to wear through.

"Come on; let's go," I urge her.

She waddles over to the door. "Okay, let's go," and slips on her boots.

We walk out the door and head to the market. Snowflakes are blowing in our faces. I cover my face trying to protect my cheeks from the cold, but Elle is making a game out of it and tries to catch the snowflakes in her mouth. We walk into the market and everyone is bundled up in winter clothes. I hear the usual chatter as we walk through the store. People are talking amongst themselves about how expensive meat cost and how fruit is scarce this time of year.

I also overheard some folks talking about wolf attacks that occurred near town. It upsets me to think there maybe another werewolf in the area and I can't warn anyone. If I say anything, they will either lock me up for being crazy or try to kill me. I pray it's just another stray wolf and not a werewolf.

On our way back home we cut through the middle of the Town Square, and people's heads turn in our direction. I assume it's because they found out that Ash and I are engaged and not that I'm a werewolf. News travels fast in a small town. I hear giggling and look in the direction of two girls staring at me with revulsion. I recognize them immediately. They once were friends with Victoria. Elle sees them and sticks her tongue out. They look disgusted and turn away. Elle nods to herself with satisfaction. When adults stare at us, Elle keeps her head down. She knows it isn't respectful to stick your tongue out at grown-ups.

I feel confident about my relationship with Ash. I fought for it and being with him is my reward. My father and Liam tried to choose a life for me and that didn't end well for them. Being with Ash is my choice and that's what I've always wanted; to make my own decisions of who I want to be with. At that moment, I made a promise to myself to never get involved in Elle's relationships.

We're almost home when I hear a thump. "Ouch!" Elle screams and looks behind her. A boy with black hair and bright green eyes is standing behind a small snow fort holding a snowball. His face turns red when we both turn and see him with a bunch of snowballs at his feet. I nudge Elle.

"I think he wants to play," I whisper to her. She buries her face in my jacket, and I pull her off. "Come on, Elle, he might be your Ash," I tell her.

She looks at the ground. "But what if he is my Liam?" she asks me.

"Listen," I say as I grip her shoulders, "if he ever gives you trouble, come get me," I say.

She looks up at me. "But what about our plans we made?" she asks me.

"Forget it! Let's meet your new friend," I whisper and walk over to him with Elle staying close to my side. "Did you just throw a snowball at my sister?" I ask him. His face is bright red from the cold, and he smiles mischievously.

"Okay, anyway, this is Elle and I'm Serena. And you are?" I ask.

He swallows hard. "Hunter Stone. Elle and I are in the same grade," he says, his eyes are bright and wide. He seems nice enough. There goes my promise to keep my nose out of Elle's relationships. That pledge lasted a few seconds.

"Okay, now that we are all introduced to one another; you kids have fun. I'm headed to the house to put these groceries away and will meet you back here later."

Elle catches my arm. "Don't do anything stupid," she laughs.

"Hey, I won't if you won't," I tease back. She raises her eyebrows and turns toward Hunter. As I walk away I hear Hunter giving Elle instructions on how to pack a snowball.

After putting the groceries in the cupboards, I head towards the woods to take a short cut to Ash's house. I hesitate before entering the woods and stare at the snow-covered trees. I notice a no hunting sign nailed to a tall pine tree. I head into the woods and look for the path that I take to Ash's house. With all the fresh snow, I can't seem to locate it. As I look down walking aimlessly, I don't see the low branch until I feel it scrape across my cold face. It stings and I put my hand over the scratch and notice a blood stain on my glove. I stomp my foot out of frustration because it feels like a gouge rather than a scratch. The cold air is making it feel worse and I start to think about the ugly scar it will leave behind after it heals. I feel the anger building inside as the pain in my face throbs.

My body starts to shake. At first I think it's because of the cold wind, but then I realize it's not the cold at all. My eyes start to sting. I feel the same way I did that day I killed Liam. I stretch my arms in front of me and notice I'm changing into a werewolf. My senses are heightened and I start pacing around as I notice a strange smell. I crouch down ready for anything that might attack me.

An elderly man with raggedy clothes appears in front of me and smiles. "Hello, Serena," he says. Before I can react, he quickly turns into his werewolf form.

Who is this man and how does he know my name? I wonder to myself.

"I came to warn you. There are those that are unhappy with the way Liam died." His mouth doesn't move, but his voice still speaks to me. "They blame you and your friend Ash for taking young Liam's life."

"Liam didn't leave me a choice! He is responsible for his own death." I hear my voice box vibrating, but I don't need to move my lips for the words to be heard.

"I'm not here to hurt you. I'm just here to warn you," he says with a smile.

"Why?" I ask him.

He shakes his head. "Your father was my closest friend. He loved you girls so much and I won't be a part of this plot against you. Let me ask you something. If you knew he was your father during the attack, do you think you would have killed him?" he asks.

I realize I've never thought about it before and answer, "I don't know what I would have done."

"Bloodlines run deep. Your father was trying to protect you from a life of heartbreak. Your human friend will not survive next time." He says pacing back and forth and then stopping to stare at me with his gold eyes narrowing into slits.

We change back to human form when the threat is gone. The first thing I become aware of is the pain in my face disappeared. I rub my face and do not see a drop of blood on my hand. When I look up to continue the conversation, the man is gone.

I'm almost to Ash's house when I trip over a tree stump hidden underneath the snow. I slide a few feet in the snow scraping my hands and arms on the branches and rocks below the snow covered terrain. I scream out in frustration and pull myself to a sitting position and examine the damage. I hear the door of someone's house open, and look up to see a woman I don't recognize running towards me. She helps me into the house.

My teeth chatter uncontrollably. "My goodness child! What are you doing out in this cold weather?" she asks me.

I observe her face and she seems familiar, but I can't

figure out how I know her. "Long story," is all I say. She hands me a cup of hot tea which I gulp down until the cup is empty and finally say, "thank you."

She looks at my face like she recognizes me. "I had a son once about your age. He died recently." Her face goes blank.

"I'm sorry to hear that," I say.

She stares at me for a minute and then snaps her fingers. "You're shivering dear, I bet you're still cold," and she reaches for a blanket next to the couch and wraps it around my shoulders. "Where are you headed?" She cocks her head to the side like she's still trying to figure out who I am.

I start to answer her when I hear heavy footsteps above. "Kiana, who are you talking to?" A man's deep voice yells from upstairs.

I start to get up, but the woman touches my shoulder, and I sit back down. The man comes down the stairs, and I pull the blanket up to my chin when I recognize the man is Liam's dad! I lower my eyes and hope he won't recognize me.

"Preston, look who I found in the snow," she says as she uncovers my face. I try to look strong, but I can't help feeling trapped.

He gives me an evil smile. "Hello, Serena. Remember me? Remember Liam?" He says with fire in his eyes.

I nod and try to find the right words to say. "I'm sorry about what happened to Liam. I truly am." I see this is not what he wants to hear from the girl who killed their only son. I see his eyes start to change colors and I realize my situation went from bad to worse. I jump up and run to the door, but when I reach for the handle, I've transformed into a werewolf.

I growl at him. He is bigger than me and his fur is black with brown streaks. His teeth are yellowish and his claws are chipped.

I move close to Kiana and show my teeth. "Are you seeking revenge for Liam's death?" I ask.

His ears go back, and he growls. "Liam was our only child and you took him away from us." He stares me down and moves in closer. "I want you to pay for what you did. I want you to feel the same pain I'm feeling." I want you to live with the hole in your heart each day you wake up." His breath is warm and he steps even closer to me.

"Are you planning to kill me?" I show him my teeth again to make sure he knows that I am ready to fight at any second.

His nose scrunches, and his ears twitch. "I plan to take something away you hold close to your heart to make you suffer," he flatly says and changes back into human form.

I alter back into human form. "Stay away from Ash!" I bark.

"Be prepared to suffer," Liam's father blurts out as he turns his back on me.

"I'm really sorry about Liam." I whisper to Kiana and run outside into the cold.

I run to Ash's house and knock on the door. He answers it and looks at me; he doesn't question me until I'm inside. "What's wrong?" he asks.

"I ran into Liam's father and he's making threats against you. He's hurting because of what I did to Liam." I tell him. He puts his arm around me, and I put my head on his shoulder. We walk over to a dusty tan color couch and sit down.

A boy about thirteen walks into the room and stops in front of us. "Her? That's Serena?!" he asks in disbelief. Ash nods. "When did you become a chick magnet?" the boy says as he walks past us into the kitchen. I feel uncomfortable when he says "chick."

Ash laughs. "I'm sorry about Drew. He's my younger brother and apparently he's not around girls very much."

I glance at the boy with blonde hair and hazel eyes. His smile is wide and he has dimples. "How old are you Drew?" I question.

"Fifteen and not too young for you." he responds as he walks by me and winks. I blush.

"Hey! No hitting on my girl!" Ash yells at him and jumps up from the couch. Drew tries to dodge him, but Ash grabs his arm and pulls him to the ground.

They wrestle for a bit on the ground, and I just sit there amused. Ash eventually wins, pinning Drew to the ground, making him tap out, and they get up. Drew leaves the room. Ash sits next to me and asks about my encounter with Liam's father. "Liam's dad is very upset with me and he's going to punish me by hurting you," I tell him.

He pauses for a minute before responding, "Do you know what he has planned?" he asks.

I shake my head and say, "No, I don't know what he has planned. Be careful if you come in contact with anyone you don't know. They will try to get you when you're alone and unable to protect yourself."

Ash sets his head in my lap. "I'm not worried, I have you to protect me," he chuckles. We laugh, and I play with his hair; twisting it in my fingers.

I hear footsteps coming, but Ash doesn't lift his head

to see who it is. Ash's mother walks into the room and looks at us and clears her throat. Ash quickly sits up. She comes over to us and picks up my hand. She looks at the ring in amazement. "You're really going through with this?" she asks Ash. She glances at me.

He nods, and her eyes start watering. She doesn't say anything and walks out of the room leaving us alone again.

"She thinks we're too young," he whispers as his eyes followed where she was going.

"We are," I tell him.

"I know, but we are waiting until you turn nineteen," he reminds me. He stretches out his right hand. I hesitate for a few seconds before taking it.

He pulls me up to my feet and hands me his thick coat to wear. We say good-bye, and he kisses my cheek before I go back outside.

The wind whips against my face, and my teeth start to chatter. I head back into town to get Elle; she is having a snowball fight with Hunter. I walk over to them, and they stop. "Come on, Elle; let's go home." She hugs me and says good-bye to Hunter. He says good-bye to her, and heads off in the opposite direction.

She looks at me. "Um, Serena, where did you get that coat?" she asks me.

I try not to worry her so I tell her, "I lost my coat and Ash let me borrow his."

Elle sighs "I told you not to do anything stupid! What happened?" She looks worried and tugs at the heavy black coat.

"I didn't! Liam's dad saw me, and I turned into a werewolf. That's the stupidest thing I did today!" I plead my case.

She covers her red cheeks with her mittens, trying to warm them. "Ash has a younger brother; I wonder why he didn't mention it before," I mumble to her.

She jumps up and down squealing. "He does?! He does?! Maybe he is *my* Ash!" she squeals.

I shake my head no and she stops jumping. "I don't think you would like him. He's too old for you," I say.

When we arrive home, I sense something is wrong. I have learned to trust my instincts recently. Quickly, I shove Elle behind me and remove the coat Ash let me borrow. It seems I can't control changing into a werewolf. I feel my eyes stinging and within seconds I transform into a werewolf. Another werewolf approaches around the corner of the house. It stops when it sees me. I nudge Elle's arm with my huge shoulder, she runs into the house.

I recognize her immediately. "What brings you here?" I ask sarcastically.

"I heard that you refused to marry Liam and came over to see what the trouble was," she explains as she sits down.

I pace back and forth wondering why she decides to show up now. "I'm engaged now." She stands back up again and starts to come towards me. I blurt out before she gets too close, "Liam is dead. I'm engaged to someone else."

She stops in her tracks; her teeth exposed. "You what!?" her voice is louder than before.

I take a step back and repeat. "I am engaged to someone else. Liam is dead, because I killed him," I emphasize the word killed.

She takes a step back and sits down with her head dropped. "On accident, right?" she asked concerned.

"No, he was about to kill my fiancée, so I killed him first." I show her my teeth so she can see that I'm serious.

She stands back up and paces around me before making a request. "Meet me in the woods at five. "And bring him." She commands.

"You want me to bring Ash to meet you in the woods at five?" I ask her. She starts to transform into human.

"Yes."

I shake my head. "No," I shout at her. "I know what you're going to do. Liam warned me about your plans to kill Ash."

Her eyes close and I watch as she transforms into a human. "Ash is his name? Adorable, really. Serena, I'm warning you. If you won't bring Ash to the woods at five, then" – she breaks off mid-sentence and turns away from me. "You and Liam were meant to be together, and that's how it should be." I watch her walk away until she disappears into the woods.

What does she mean? My ears go back, and I change back to human. Elle comes out of the house. By the terrified look on her face, I can tell she knows that something is wrong. "What's going on?" she whimpers.

"I don't know," I say honestly. I have less than three hours to come up with a plan to save Ash. I tell Elle to stay in the house until I return. I hear the door lock behind me when I slip on Ash's coat to keep me warm. I need to warn Ash and take off running as fast as I can toward his house.

CHAPTER 8

I knock on the back door of Ash's house and hear someone yell. Drew opens the door. "Hey, Drew. I need to talk to Ash," I tell him.

"Sorry, he's taking a bath," he answers. I hear a shriek and look inside. No one is there. "He's upstairs. Since its winter and we have no hot water, it's freezing!" Drew says, smiling. "You can come in." He opens the door wider and moves to the side. I step in, and it's quiet other than Ash's whimpers from his cold bath.

Drew rolls his eyes. "Ash, you need to man up! You're seriously embarrassing!" he yells to him from the bottom of the stairs. "Oh, and by the way, Serena is here!"

The sounds stop, and I hear splashing. I'm guessing Ash is getting out; there is a long pause, and then Ash comes down the stairs wearing dark jeans and pulling on a white shirt over his wet hair. The water soaks through his shirt causing it to cling tightly to his chest. "Hey, Kiwi, long-time no see!" He comes over and hugs me.

"Kiwi?" I ask him. I wipe the cold water off me that dripped from his wet hair after the hug.

"Yeah, cute nickname, huh?" he smiles. I savor his

smile because I know it will disappear once I tell him the news.

"Yeah. Anyway, I have something bad to tell you. I'm not going through with it, though," I stutter, trying to find the right words.

He drops his head, and his face gets red. "I'm confused. You're not going through what? The wedding?" he asks.

I put my hand on his soggy shoulder. "No, I am. It's just that, um … my mother wants to meet you in the woods at five o' clock today so she can kill you." I choke out the words. I'm surprised when Ash chuckles. "Why are you laughing?" I ask.

"Doesn't everybody?" he says with a laugh.

Drew laughs a bit, and I give him a look that says shut up. He stops laughing and looks away. Ash gently pushes his face against mine, and we gaze into each other's eyes. He knows that I'm not joking, but he finds something funny in it. "Did you miss the part about my mother wants to kill you? We need to figure out what to do next." I say with a serious tone. Ash stops laughing; his brown eyes widen.

Ash doesn't know what to say, and neither do I; we just stand there in silence looking at each other until Drew interrupts the quiet by clearing his throat loudly. I look at him, but Ash still continues looking at me. "Why don't I go instead of Ash. Your mother hasn't met Ash and will think I'm Ash." He says in a brave tone.

"No, you stay here. I'll go," Ash says.

I put my hand on Ash's mouth stopping him from saying anymore. "Wait, that's not a bad idea Drew had. We can find someone to pretend to be you! It will work!" I try to convince him.

I'm starting to believe this will work and everyone will be safe that I care about. Ash throws his hands in the air, and I pull my hand back. "So what? You just lead a stranger into the woods with you and watch your mom maul him?" Ash kicks the door.

"I don't want to do it either, but your life will be saved if this works," I tell him.

He rests his head on the door. "But what if it doesn't? What if she finds out? Mine, Drew's and who knows how many others' lives will be lost," he whispers.

"That won't happen," I assure him. "All I need to do is to find someone to go into the woods with me," I think out loud. I have a good—no, great—idea. I grab Ash's arm—well, as much of it as I can fit my fingers around—and pull at him. "I know how to do this!" I say with enthusiasm. Ash doesn't say anything; he just let's me lead him to the door.

We reach the door, and he stops me. "I hope you're right and this plan works." He kisses me on the lips.

I pull away and say, "I need to see Elle first." I turn toward the door.

"We don't have time for that," Ash protests and grabs my arm. "You will see her soon."

"Fine," I say, and Ash opens the door for me.

When we step outside, I shiver. Ash puts his arm around me; we walk to the middle of the square, and I turn to him. "Here," I say, taking off my ring. "Hold onto this until we meet again." I plop the beautiful ring into his hands. He grasps it and puts it in his pocket.

"We're running out of time." he says nervously.

I nod. "I think it's best if you leave me to do this by myself. I don't want to scare off any potential victims." I look over his shoulder and search for someone who could be mistaken for Ash.

"It won't take long. You'll attract someone in no time," Ash whispers.

I wish I could hug him, but I really need to find a guy and hugging Ash would send the wrong message. We say good-bye, and I watch Ash walk away.

About five minutes later, tall, brown-haired boy with brown eyes comes up to me. Ash was right; it didn't take long. "Hi," I call to him.

"Hey, um, aren't you with that Ash kid?" he asks me.

I grit my teeth, and look back to see if Ash is gone. "Uh, no. Hey, you look familiar! Where have I seen you?" I ask him, even though I don't know him.

He smiles. "I'm Jake. You probably recognize me from school."

I nod and just play along. We chat about school and the weather for several minutes. "Hey, um, I would like to get to know you better, but I need to get home to check on my little sister. Would you like to walk me home?" I ask with excitement.

"Really? Cool! Sure, let's go!" He grabs my arm and I point to the woods up ahead. We continue to talk and the more he tells me about his personal life, the more I start to regret my plan. I want to tell him to run in the opposite direction, but I don't. This is for Ash.

After a few minutes of dodging snow covered trees we stop to take a breath. He laughs, and so do I. "I didn't know that you were fun! I thought you were always a stick in the mud, but you aren't!" he says, laughing some more. I swallow hard and force a smile.

"I don't think I've ever been called fun. I've been

called strange by some." We both laugh until we hear twigs crack and snow crunching in the near distance. Behind Jake I see my mother's eyes peaking out between two trees. I wonder what to do, and I start to panic. "Good-bye, Ash!" I say as dramatically as I can. Before I take off, I need to make sure my mother buys that Jake is Ash. Jake looks at me confused and starts to say that he isn't Ash, and before he can get the words out, I grab his shirt, pull him close, and press my lips against his. *Very persuasive, I'm so going to pull this off!* I tell myself.

The kiss is passionate and Jake wraps his arms around me trying to make it last longer than I wanted. I break away from him and the guilt rips into my soul until tears slip from my eyes. I feel really horrible for leading the boy to death. I kiss his cheek and let him go. "I'm sorry," I whisper and turn around. I can't watch him die. He starts to follow me, but my mother leaps out from behind the trees.

I hear him scream something, but I don't know what. More tears roll down my face as I hear a thump noise.

I stop in my tracks when I hear blood curdling screams through the ripping of flesh from my mother's teeth and claws. I start to feel regret with my plan to save Ash. My stomach is tied in knots and it feels like I'm choking.

I feel something warm and sticky on the back of my hair and neck. I reach back and feel something in my hair. My fingers are covered in blood. Innocent blood spilt because of me. I see an empty metal snare sticking out of the snow. Someone set it out to trap an animal. A light breeze sends chills down my back as I reach down and pick it up. I turn around and with all my strength I throw it at my mother. She stops and looks at me as it barely grazed her back. My hair blows in my face, and at that moment I feel empowered. I will not let my mother or anyone else destroy my life or anyone else.

I start to run at my mother who is standing over Jake. My eyes start to sting and before I reach my mother I turn into a werewolf and leap on top of her back. I see Jake trying to defend himself, with chunks of flesh missing from his arms. He's lost so much blood that his body is shaking uncontrollably, and his eyes roll to the back of his head.

"Maybe you should pick on someone in your own species. Someone like me!" I snarl at her. Before she has a chance to respond, I bite into her neck. She howls with pain and shakes me off. But she doesn't do it quickly enough when I take another chunk out of her back. I fling the chunk of flesh to the ground, and blood is pouring out from the wound and down her furry body.

My ears go back, and my eyes narrow. She is trying to soothe the wound on her neck by licking it. She lifts her head and howls in pain. I stand there trying to figure out my next move and step back when my mother transforms back into a human. I use this opportunity to leap at her again. I snap down on her arm and shake her around until her arm is torn off. She screams and kicks at me. I pull her down to the ground and hit her jaw with my claws. I hear her jaw crack and I look into her eyes to see she is in pain. I back off and she stands up; before she takes a step, I charge her and she slam her against a tree.

She is weak, and can barely move. With all my energy I swing my paw at her head, and it cracks. I can see she is still breathing, but close to death that she's not a threat anymore. I turn back into human form and run over to

Jake. He is breathing faintly, and his eyes are wide and scared.

"I'm so sorry." I plead. I can see by his injuries, he is going to die soon, so I don't bother to ease my conscience with asking his forgiveness.

"Am I going to die," he asks in a pained voice and coughs up blood. I look away from him, and tears roll down my face. I feel a sudden sharp pain in my back and wince. I reach behind to feel blood pouring down my back. I turn around and see the metal snare on the ground with my blood on the sharp teeth. I watch my mother smile deviously at me. I pick up the snare with both hands and hurl it at her. I watch it plunge into her chest. It goes all the way in, and she falls to the ground. I hope this time, the metal teeth cut her heart to pieces.

I look back at Jack, he is nearly dead. I lift his head an inch above the ground, and cradle him.

I hear footsteps, and for the first time since I changed back, I'm cold. Ash comes out behind some trees and sees me. "Are you hurt?" he asks, looking around at Jake and my mother.

He bends down and takes Jake's head out of my hand and tells me he's gone. He helps me up and wraps his arms around me and then quickly jerks them back when his hands touch the blood on my back. "Let's go. You're bleeding," he says and picks me up in his arms. He is warm, and I try to keep my eyes open but I finally stop resisting. Everything went black.

"Serena? Can you hear me? Serena, wake up!" Ash's voice rings in my ears.

My eyelashes flutter open, and he tries to shake me awake. "Serena! Wake up!" he screams, but not out of anger, out of pure concern.

I push his arms away and sit up. "I'm alive!" I say groggy.

The cut in my back has almost disappeared. My fingers search around for the huge tear in my shirt and feel the once gash, and the wound is almost gone. The only thing I feel is a scratch. "Unbelievable," I whisper.

Ash slips my ring back on my finger. "I think it's safe to put this back where it belongs," he whispers in my ear.

"Is it over?" I ask.

"Liam, your father and your mother are gone. What else is out there that can hurt us?" Ash asks.

I stare at no place in particular. "I don't know. I want this to madness to stop." I pause for a minute looking at Ash and how handsome he is. "I know this isn't the right time to ask, but how do you feel about adoption? I don't want to pass this horrific gene to another generation." My words are muffled and soft.

He takes my hair and pulls it out from underneath my neck. "I'm in favor of adopting as long as we are together. I always pictured my child with brown and brown eyes," Ash plays with my hair.

I sigh. "Why are we even talking about this?" I tell him.

He rips a piece of loose string from a pillow and ties my hair off. "I guess we want to picture a future together..." Ash stops there.

I sit up. "Ash, let's just drop the subject," I suddenly do not feel like talking about kids. I take in a deep breath. "So, tomorrow we go back to school, right?" I ask.

"Sure, but a good education isn't really important around here," Ash replies as he lies down. He sinks his head into a soft pillow he pulled from the couch, and pulls me close to him. We are the only ones at his house.

"It's quiet at your house." I say, moving in closer to him to keep warm.

Ash laughs and looks around to see we are the only ones. "Well, time for you to rest some more," Ash says and wraps his arm around my waist.

I look at the clock. It's midnight. I lie next to him and close my eyes.

CHAPTER 9

I wake to the smell of food cooking.

I sit up and see Ash's mother cooking breakfast. I was right—eggs frying and cups of water on the table. She sees me and says good morning.

"Good morning, Mrs. Parker. I'm just leaving, so please tell Ash that I'm all right," I tell her. She nods and gives me an egg. I thank her and walk outside.

The sun is out, the snow is starting to melt, and the ground is mushy. I step in squishy grass, and my foot gets stuck. I pull it out and continue walking for home.

I open the front door and step in. I head straight for my room and slam the door. I pull off my old clothes and replace them with new ones. I am wearing a white-and-black sweater with a pair of dark-colored jeans.

I step out of the room and see Elle coming out of her room. Groggy and tired, she makes her way over to me.

"Elle, Ash and I are headed back to school today. Do you want to come?" I ask her. She shakes her head and goes back in her room. "You should!" But I don't force her. I'm not sure if that makes me irresponsible, but I've had that attitude for over six years and Elle and I turned out fine. Well, at least Elle did.

I hear her fall on the bed. I can tell that she is asleep. I hurry and brush my teeth and hair. I swipe whatever pair of socks that are in front of me at that second, pull on my boots, and run out the door. I see Ash walking to school, and I catch up to him. "Hey, Ash!" I say.

"Hey, Kiwi. How's everything?" He looks at me.

"Fine, you?" I respond.

He shrugs. "Nothing much. Are you ready to face everyone at school?" he asks me with concern. Once again, he's concerned about me.

"Yes. It's not like everyone is going to stare and point when we walk by," I assure him. He nods, and we make it to school without another word.

Once we enter the school yard, everyone watches us walk by. Some even whisper. I feel like an outsider, and I can't even begin to imagine what Ash is thinking. The bell rings, and everyone scatters. I feel a drop of rain on my sleeve, then another and another. Pretty soon it starts to rain. In about thirty seconds my hair and clothes are soaked. Ash's hair gets in his face, and I push it aside.

The rain doesn't bother me. I hold my head to the sky and open my mouth. I let the rain drip in; it's sweet and cold. Ash does the same. The last bell rings, and we are all alone. I begin to walk in the direction everyone else is going but Ash stops me. I put my head down and Ash mimics me. I go into his arms, and he is just as wet as I am. His blue shirt is dripping, and his jeans are soaked. My white-and-black sweater and jeans are wet. I hear thunder and jump.

Ash pulls me closer, and I throw my arms around his

neck. I pull my head back so I can look into his eyes. We stare at each other for a moment and then he pulls me into a kiss. My eyes open, and I see a few kids looking through a window at us. I close my eyes again. Ash backs up and turns his head to cough.

"What?" I ask.

"Your hair got caught in my mouth," he says, gagging. The kids from the window are laughing now.

"Oh thanks for gagging on my hair!" I say defensively as I check it out; it's long and tangled now. "Come on we need to get inside." I tell him after he is done getting my hair out of his mouth.

"Sure," he says and pushes more hair out of my face. He smiles at me and moves in closer to me. I push him back with a smile, and dash toward the doors. "Hey, what's the big idea?" Ash calls, chasing after me into the brown brick building.

I stop and turn around. "What do you think? I'm going to class," I tell him and head to my locker. I take out my history book and notebook and walk to class. I try to avoid eye contact with anyone as I make my way to class. History is boring along with the rest of the seven hours of school since I didn't see Ash once.

When the final bell rings to release the students, Ash and I meet up by the gym. We run out the back doors and into the misty rain. We sit down on top of a hill that overlooks the field across from the school. Ash wobbles.

"Oh no! I'm slipping!" he screams as he slides down the grass. He grabs my ankle and pulls me with him.

"Ash, no!" I shriek. But I can't help it; I laugh on the way down. We stop at the bottom in soggy golden-brown leaves. We laugh for about five minutes then stop. I hear a roar in the distance.

Ash grabs my wrist. "Run!" he cries and pulls me away. I free myself and run towards the noise. "Not again!" I hear him say.

My eyes are stinging and I feel myself changing into a werewolf. I see a bobcat at the edge of the tree line looking at me. As I approach it, I growl and snarl at it. I make sure to show all of my teeth and snap at it. Its ears go back, and it runs away. I change back into human form and walk back to where I left Ash.

Even thought the temperature has warmed up a bit and the rain has melted most of the snow, I'm a little cold when I change back to human form. "You really have to stop changing at every little growl you hear!" Ash says to me.

"Eventually," I tell him. As we walk to no place in particular, I spot the tree on the edge of woods that I used to climb when Liam came after me. I point and run for it.

Ash follows me until we reach the tree. I start climbing up, but a stain of blood on a low branch distracts me—my blood. I think back to that night when Liam hit the side of my face and I shiver.

I press two fingers against my cheek and feel where the wound use to be. Ash senses my uneasiness and asks what's wrong. I snap back into reality. "This was my escape tree. I came here whenever Liam ran after me," I whisper.

Ash holds onto a branch and pulls himself up. "Well, that won't happen again. Come up," he says and stretches out his hand to me. I take it, and he pulls me up.

We climb higher and higher until we find a perfect fork of branches to rest in. "This is also where Liam saved my life. Liam wasn't lying when he told you he caught me from falling," I tell him.

He turns to me. "I thought he was just making that up! He really did save your life?" he asks.

I nod and continue. "After he set me down, he hit the side of my face. Right here," I say, pointing to the barely visible scar. Ash climbs out farther and lies back on a thick branch. I wedge myself between a solid branch and the trunk before closing my eyes. The branches protect us from the rain and the sound of raindrops sings me to sleep.

I know I'm dreaming, but I can't wake up. I see myself in a striped sleeveless shirt with jeans standing in the forest. I notice that Liam is there wearing a black shirt and black shorts. I run to him and hug his neck; it's warm and sticky. I back up and see my arms are covered in blood. He has a blank expression on his face.

"You did this. If I were still alive, Ash would be out of harm. But you're too selfish to see that," Liam spits the words into my face. I feel terrible but remember that it is only a dream. I have control of what I say, so I speak what I think.

"I miss you a lot, and I'm sorry. I can't undo what I already did," I tell him.

"Or can you?" Liam asks me. "All you have to do is kill Ash." He walks toward me, and I take a step back.

"Never! You're dead!" I yell. He keeps on walking, and I finally stop backing up. He walks right through me, and I turn around.

"As far as you know," he whispers and disappears.

CHAPTER 10

I wake up and see the rain has stopped. Birds are perched on branches singing tranquil melodies. I look to my right; Ash is still sleeping. Careful not to wake him, I stand up on the branch. Some of the birds scatter for a minute but then come back.

In a low voice, I sing. "Remember the place where there is peace? Remember the place where there was calm? Remember the soft green grass or the flowing river? This is a place of joy, and this is a place of dreams. This is the place where we belong; this is the place for our song. Remember all the crazy things we said and stupid things we've done? Remember all the stars we wished on or the big oak tree we sat upon? This is a place of tears, and this is a place of pain. This is a place where we don't belong; this is the place for our song." As my voice trails off, I trace broken pieces of bark on the trunk with my finger and think of Liam.

I glance at Ash—still fast asleep. In the distance I hear a gunshot and people cheering. I look through some of the branches and needles to find about five or so men with a deer. I roll my eyes.

I squint and see a bottle of something in a short man's

hand. Whisky or liquor is the first thing to pop into my mind. Danger—drunk hunters are the worst kind of people in Pine Hill.

I turn my back against the trunk and keep still. Ash wakes up and climbs to the branch next to me. "Morning, Kiwi!" he says enthusiastically. I press my hand against his mouth, but I know it's too late. The men stop cheering and look around. *Please don't find us, please don't find us!* I pray silently, Ash looks confused until he sees the men. He presses up against the trunk and I let my hand down.

We watch them as they pass right in front of us. One of them takes a swig from the bottle. "What do you think was out there?" he asks, his voice slurred and shaky.

Another man hits him upside the head. "Shut up! You might scare it away! It could be game; now shut up!" he yells.

The man with the bottle smiles at the other man. "You just scared it off with your yelling!" he laughs as he falls to the ground.

Ash leans next to my ear. "If anyone offers me a drink and I say yes, please slap me," he whispers.

"Will do," I say, and we turn our attention to the hunters again. The man who is seriously drunk and the one who just yelled at him are now wrestling.

"Who do you think will win?" Ash asks, keeping his voice low.

"Drunken guy doesn't stand a chance. He'll probably be bloodied in less than two minutes," I reply. Ash nods and holds onto a branch above us.

I was right; the drunken man has a bloody nose, and I'm not sure, but I think one of his teeth just flew out of his mouth. "Let's go to the other side," Ash says and puts a foot on a branch to his right. I mimic his movements, but unfortunately, my boot slips. I fall until my hands catch a branch; I grip on to it.

Ash grabs my hands and pulls me up. The men start looking around the tree. I see they are both carrying a knife and a gun. Ash and I lean against the trunk as close as possible and don't make a sound. Blood drips from the cuts on my arms and legs where the branches hit me, but I'm not worried about it, because it'll heal swiftly enough. The hunter with the spear looks our way and points. Ash and I freeze.

"I see something!" he calls. Each man pushes the other one out of his way to get a better look.

"There's nothing up there, you brainless idiot! But if you want to waste a bullet to try and get it, be my guest!" the man standing next to the drunk yells. I hear my heart pound as I watch the man aim his gun at me.

"Ash, head to the other side," I command him.

"What about you?" he asks.

"There's nothing I can't heal from," I tell him. He refuses to go without me and drags me with him. I hear the gunshot and feel the bullet graze my left arm. I wince, and Ash stops. He looks at my arm; a gash of missing flesh and muscles the size of the bullet bleeds heavily.

"See, nothing's up there, numb skull! You just wasted a bullet. Let's go!" the hunter screams.

"Wait, I always double check," the man who shot me says and walks under the needles. He holds out his hand, and I know what he's doing. I always do this when I'm not sure if I hit something up high. I hold my cut, but blood drips through my fingers. When the drops land on the man's arms, he yells for the rest of them to come and see.

He looks up and sees me and Ash standing there; the others follow his gaze. "You didn't hit an animal. You just hit these kids you—"

"Hey," Another man yells. "Isn't that the girl everyone is talking about?"

What? Who's talking about me? Why? And what are they saying? I wonder to myself, but I don't ask. I just hold onto my arm, and Ash tries to stop the blood. The only thing I can think to do is kick my shoe off at them. It hits the drunk, and he falls to the ground. Everyone laughs, even Ash. This time I don't kick my shoe off. I take it off and aim it at another one of the men. I chuck it, and it hits him in the side of the head.

"Ash, if you have a weapon, let me see it," I demand. He digs through his back pockets but finds nothing, same results with the front pockets.

One man starts climbing up the tree. Once he's close enough, I kick him as forcefully as possible. He falls down, but grabs a branch before he manages to hit the ground. Unfortunately, the branch snaps and he rolls onto the ground. I have taken care of them all, the drunk I hit with my shoe, I hit another with my shoe, and kicked one out of a tree.

The others ran off a few seconds ago with the man I hit with my shoe. There's the man I just sliced, and the other is scared out of his wits.

I snap my jaws at him, and he runs away. Ash smiles. "Wimps," he murmurs under his breath. The others begin to regain consensus. I have no more shoes left, so Ash takes his off and hits some of them in the face. I admit his shots were pretty accurate, but nothing close to what I can do. The men run out of the tree and into the woods.

My arm is already starting to heal; the muscles are healed, and the skin is just barely coming back. The blood has stopped. Ash slides his hand down my arm into my hand.

"Ash, its fine," I tell him. He releases my hand and we climb down. "That was terrifying! Let's never sleep in a tree again," I say, and he agrees. A painful pounding in my ears begins; I cover them, but the noise grows; preventing me from blocking it out completely.

"What is that?" Ash asks me. I have no idea, the only thing I concentrate on now is trying to get the sound out of my head until I realize that it's coming from back of me.

I turn and see a large polished black helicopter with a huge B painted on the side hovering above. It looks like its searching for something. After awhile, it flies over the woods and then heads toward town.

Ash and I remain still, but I can't help feeling like Ash and I were what it was looking for. After all, our town is filled with demons and mythical creatures.

I slide my hand into Ash's and cling to his side. "What is with the helicopter? Do you think they are looking for someone?" he whispers and looks at me as if I have an answer.

I don't want to tell Ash they might be looking for him because they think he's insane for his gossip mouth at the hospital about Victoria. I shrug and say without alarm, "I don't know. I'm sure they have a good reason." I surprise myself how jaded I sound when I'm really curious about it too. Ash sighs and puts his arm around me.

"They come here almost never and for some reason show up…" he looks back into the trees. "Doesn't it seem strange, that they would just show up out of the blue?"

The pounding starts again. "No." I answer too quickly and Ash's eyes fall back on me once more looking confused. I shake my head slightly and dig my fingernail into my hand for being so stupid. "I mean, yes it is strange," Ash looks down at my arms.

"Are you cold? You're shaking." He wraps his arms around me. I wince when he touches the bullet wound. Ash moves his arms lower to avoid the wound before apologizing.

I didn't realize I was shaking until Ash brought it up. I force myself to stop shaking and snuggle closer to Ash.

"It's just a helicopter Serena, it doesn't mean something bad happened." he tells me in a calm soothing voice.

"As far as you know nothing bad happened," I say in a breathless whisper. Liam's voice rings in my ear with the same phrase, 'as far as you know.'

"What did you say?" Ash asks me. "Is there something you're keeping from me?" When I don't respond, he walks away.

At first it feels nice to finally be alone. But after the minutes drag slowly past, I begin to get lonely and crave his company.

I take off in the same direction to find him. As I get further into the woods, I don't know which way to turn, so I run straight forward. I stop when I come to an open field. Quietly, I walk to where he lays facing the blue skies with his hands behind his head.

I lie down next to him and face toward the sky. "Hey," I say as I watch a puffy cloud float by. I glance at him to see if he's still mad at me. I can't read his expression so I turn away.

Ash sighs. "Three years," he mumbles.

"You say it like it's a bad thing," I say.

He looks at me, but I still face the sky. "You don't think it is?" he asks.

I shrug. "I don't know, maybe. I want to be with you forever married or not."

"I want to be with you forever, but I don't know if forever will be a long time considering all that we are dealing with!" Ash argues. I've never heard Ash's use that tone with me before.

My eyes sting; I'm afraid I'll turn werewolf again, but tears come instead. Refusing to cry, I blink rapidly and suck in a deep breath. "I don't like it anymore than you, but this is who I am!" I choke out.

Ash huffs and sits up. I see his cheeks are turning a light red. "Don't you think I know who you are?" he asks with an edge to his tone.

I stand up and throw my hands in the air. "Are you sure in three years you're not going to regret being married to a werewolf wife?" I ask.

Ash stands up. "What?" He tries hard to conceal his anger.

"Be honest with yourself!" I blurt out. I watch as Ash's hands turn into fists and slightly jerk forward. Naturally, I jump back and shut my eyes. I quickly open my eyes and stare at Ash in disbelief. "You were actually going to hit me!" I stand up and run for the woods with tears rolling down my cheeks. I turn around before Ash is out of sight and yell, "You're just like Liam!"

I stop and bury my face inside my hands. Our first fight—and I don't know if it's our last. I try to rub off the dried blood on my hands using the smooth bark from a birch tree. Ash runs up to me. "Serena, I-I don't really know what to say."

I stop him and shout the words into his face. "I do. We're through!" With that, I run off again, trying to get away from him. He doesn't follow me this time; he just stays there looking down at the ground. I decide not to go home and explain everything to Elle.

Maybe I was meant to be with Liam. I hate to admit it, but I miss him a lot. If he were still alive would Ash and I still be friends? Most likely not; Liam's jealousy would prevent us from being friends.

My head starts to spin, and my legs feel like jelly. I fall into dead wet leaves surrounding a tall maple tree. I can't focus on anything right now. I try to remember when was the last time I had something to eat. The last things I see are stars as darkness starts to overcome me. I can't even cry for help. I blackout!

At first, I feel at peace when I fade into the blackness. But then, my mind starts to create scenarios that include being dragged away and eaten by a bear. I have some sense of consciousness, because I know I'm vulnerable and unprotected. Anything can happen to me. I'm just too confused and upset to care. Maybe I deserve to die after what I've done to Liam, my father and my mother. It would make everyone's lives easier if I were dead. Maybe that's what I need to do; I'll run away from everything and build a new life.

I think about my plan for about three seconds and find one flaw. Build it out of what? With no Elle or Ash in my life, what will become of me and them? I guess I don't really have a plan after all.

CHAPTER 11

I wake to the sound of hushed high pitched voices over my face.

"Do you think she's dead?" one voice asks.

"No. Look, she's breathing. A dead person doesn't breathe, Smarts!"

"I know her!" another one squeals.

"No you don't!" another one shouts.

I open my eyes, and three little kids are sitting on their knees next to me. "Told ya she's not dead!" a boy with blonde hair and blue eyes says.

"So I guess you're not entirely stupid," the red-headed girl says back. The little girl with strawberry blonde hair and freckles covering her face just sits and looks at me.

"Who are you guys?" I ask.

They scoot closer to me. "What happened to you?" the redhead asks me.

I shake my head. "I think I passed out from not eating," I tell them.

"Oh!" the boy says. "I have an apple in my pocket you can have."

"That's nice of you. I'm sure it will help me feel better."

The kids gasp. "You have blood on you!" the strawberry blonde girl points to my hands.

I sigh and try to come up with a lie of why I'm bloody. "I'm ok. I cut myself on a bear trap before I passed out." I say.

"I only see dried blood, but no cut," the little girl says, and her blue eyes get big.

"I bleed easy and the cut is small. I'm really doing fine."

The girl leans over me and whispers. "Are you sure?"

I'm not doing fine. I think. *I want Ash, I want my old life back, I want to be normal.* I think of Liam and what our future might have been like. Ash would be safe, but Elle would be miserable. I think of her huddling in a corner trying to escape mine and Liam's fights every day. I couldn't live with myself if anything happened to her.

The boy holds out the apple and I sit up and eat it quickly. I thank them for helping me and start running for home. I see our house and run faster until I reach the door. When trying to open the locked door I smell smoke. "Elle!" I scream and pound on the door.

"Serena!" she calls.

I stop banging on the door and listen. By the sound of her cry, she is in trouble. "Elle, don't worry. I'm coming!" I scream. I kick the door and slam myself into it over and over again until it breaks the hinges.

I rush in and see the house is full of smoke and the outline of the house is burning. "Elle, I'm in! Where are you?" I scream.

"Over here!" she calls from the middle of the living

room. I run toward her cries and feel through the thick smoke with my arms outstretched. I see her face and she is reaching out for me crying to save her. I start after her, and she cries harder. Just before I reach her, a piece of the burning ceiling collapses onto her.

"Elle!" I scream and rush over to her.

I hear her cough. I yank the wood off her and pick her up. Her body isn't burnt, but it's dirty with ashes. I look around for an escape route; the flames engulf us. My eyes start to water from the smoke and the heat from the flames are burning my skin.

"Help! Help!" I shout, but the only thing I hear is the crackle of the fire. I hear a window shatter. I run over to it and knock out the sharp edges. I kiss Elle's forehead, and carefully help her out the window which she barely fits through.

The space is too small for me to fit through. I look franticly around for an opening to escape the burning flames. When I can't find one, I sink to my knees and cry. I peek through my fingers to look at my ring; it sparkles with red and orange. The flames are quickly eating away at the floorboards and creeping toward my body.

I close my eyes and pray. "Please don't let me die. I will do anything to live," I whisper and take my face out of my hands just in time to watch a board fall from the ceiling.

I squeeze my eyes shut and wait for the painful sting of the flames. I feel something jump on top of me to protect me form the falling ceiling. I hear a yelp and then realize it's a werewolf. He nudges me and I hop on his back and he takes off through the smoke and doesn't stop until we are safely outside.

I open my eyes and see a brown werewolf dump me

gently onto the ground. I'm speechless and can't believe this is the same werewolf who warned me in the woods about plans to kill Ash. I'm overjoyed with making it out alive and stand up. The fire is being put out by some people I don't know. I watch the werewolf transform into a human and take off to help the others to put out the fire.

The air is heavy with smoke and I look around to see Elle running towards me. She hugs me and I hug her back. I pull her arms away from my waist and make my way to the people after they finish putting out the fire to thank them.

I start to put my arms around the man with a scruffy beard and black hair but he pushes me away. "You said that you would do anything to live. The wolves want a child within the next two years," the man stares down at me.

I'm speechless once more. I step back into a pile of burnt debris. "What are you talking about?" I ask him. He continues to stare at me without saying anything. "I'm not even married!" I shout at him.

He smiles at me and so does the woman standing next to him. "All right," he says. "Once you're married, we will be expecting you to carry on the next generation. Do we have an understanding?"

I toss that idea around in my head for a bit and think this must be a joke so I play along. "I only want to have one," I chuckle. "I don't want a whole pack to take care of. I hope it's a boy because…" The woman cuts me off mid-sentence.

"You are destined to have a daughter. The arrangements have been made for her and Hunter." she says.

My mouth drops open, and I stare at her. "Hunter Stone? No, that can't be." I protest. "Hunter is eight years old!" I add.

He tilts his head and nods. "It's predestined, you can't change it." He straightens his shoulders. "Just like you're destined to be with your chosen mate," he says.

He puts his hand on my shoulder and lightly squeezes. "Do you understand Serena? He doesn't wait for me to answer when he pulls away and grabs the woman's arm and they walk away.

I sit down on top of the debris and put my face in my ash covered hands. My house is half burnt, my little sister is scared to death, and I'm starting to realize I have no control over my own life.

I hear Elle call my name and I look up as she approaches. "I'm not sure how to tell you this," I pause and look down at the ground.

She looks at me with concern. "What? What happened?" she asks.

I take in a deep breath and let it out slowly. "Hunter Stone is a werewolf and is destined to marry my daughter," I tell her.

"But you don't have a daughter." she says. Her voice is raspy from the smoke.

"I know, but I just found out that I will have a daughter in the near future, and," I take in another deep breath, "She will not have a choice in who she will be with, just like me."

I notice my hands start shaking. I look down. "I can't believe this is my life! I can't believe this will be the life of my child!" I can't help but scream.

Elle's brown eyes bulge. "You are going to be with

Ash! You made that happen!" she shrieks. I nod and look at her. She is still, and I see goose bumps on her arms.

"I'm sorry Elle. I feel like I'm letting you down. The mangy wolves are calling the shots and they want me to produce an offspring. I thought about adopting so I can stop this generation of freaks. I'm afraid if I don't comply with their demands, they may start taking away what really matters to me." I pull her down to meet her eyes. "You matter," I whisper.

She sits next to me, and I start crying. "Don't. Don't do it," she tries to comfort me, as if that's an option.

"No. No, I have to. If I don't, you and Ash will pay for it!" I wrap my arm around her and pull her chilled body next to me.

"At least you'll be happy," she says and shrugs her shoulders.

"All of us Elle. Don't you get it? They will kill all of us!" I wail. "I can't protect you from everything! This was way too close!" I yell. She hugs me, and I bury my face in her neck. "Why are they doing this to me?" I whisper into her shoulder.

She pats my head. "Who knows? Maybe you'll like your new life," Elle suggests. Am I being selfish—everyone will be safe if I do what they ask. No, I won't be a puppet. No, I won't produce another generation of freaks. And no, I will not let them control what happens in my life! I just need a plan.

How do I protect both Ash and Elle? I can't spend all of my time running back and forth, protecting them from the wolves. I can't choose one over the other. There's only one solution.

"Elle," I whisper to her with tears filling up in my eyes.

"I'm going to break up with Ash." I break our hug and start choking on my tears, trying not to let Elle see them. "I love him, but you're more important to me," I say.

"You shouldn't have to choose. I want you to stay with him." She takes my arm and squeezes it.

"You're in danger and I can't be with you all the time to protect you," I say, and she puts a finger to my lips.

"Don't talk about it. Now go find Ash," she tells me.

I sniffle and hug her again. "I won't abandon you. We won't be separated if Ash is out of our lives!" I wince.

She nudges my head. "I'm sorry this is happening to you," she mumbles into my hair. I squeeze her one last time and get up.

My nose starts to run, but I wipe it off with my hand. I walk away from the smoldering house and from Elle. I wipe the tears out of my eyes continually, because they refuse to stop flowing. I arrive at Ash's house and wipe my eyes one more time before I knock. He answers it and sees my face. He comes outside and shuts the door behind him.

"What is it?" he asks.

"We can't be together. It's too dangerous for you and for Elle," I tell him. "I hate to ask this, but can you come with me to say goodbye to Elle?" He nods his head and hesitates before holding my hand.

We walk in silence until we reach the house, and I push what's left of the burnt door open. Elle is lying on the floor and sobbing. I try to comfort her. My tears start to flow and they flood my eyes again. I help her up to her feet and look directly at her. Her eyes are pink, and her face is red.

"Listen, you take care of yourself okay? Always

remember the most important thing while I'm gone—I will always love you like you were my real sister," Ash's voice cracks as he speaks. He hugs her tight.

Elle looks at me and then at Ash. "And I love you like a brother," she says. "I know we will be seeing each other again soon." With that, she starts sobbing.

Ash's face is red, and I can see that he is trying to hold back tears.

"I want to spend some alone time with Ash and I will be back soon and we will start cleaning up this place." I say. She nods and hugs me one last time. "I love you," I whisper, and we let go.

"I love you too, Serena!" she calls as Ash and I head out the door. I blow her a kiss and walk out.

I shut the door and fall into Ash's arms. He catches me and tries to calm me down. We walk for an hour in a random direction. "She's all I got." I blurt out.

Ash strokes my head. "No she's not. You have me," he says resting his chin on my head.

"Where do we go now?" I ask him looking up.

"I don't know. The woods maybe?" he says.

I sniff and wipe my nose again. "We could go to your river," I suggest. He nods, and we continue on. We push through sagging trees and overgrown bushes until the river is in sight. I stop at the water and watch my reflection in the ripples. Everything seems gloomy, lifeless, dead.

"Why am I even alive?" I ask myself. "I don't deserve to be." I pick up a smooth pebble and throw it into the river. I watch it sink and think of my life is like that rock. It's sinking to the bottom of darkness.

Ash comes up behind me. "There's got to be something we can do to stay together." he stammers.

I look at him with a hopeless stare. I want to tell him I love him, but it will make it harder, so I just lay my head on his shoulder and start crying. "I hate this!" I yell.

Ash stiffens up and my head slips off his shoulder. I look at his face and he is staring straight ahead into the trees.

"Ash," I say. But he keeps focusing on the trees. "Ash, what is it?" I ask sternly. He ignores me. I look towards the trees and see three figures coming in our direction.

As they come closer, I see they are teenage boys about our age or a little older. I see the tallest boy point at us and mouth something, but I can't hear what he is saying, but I can see he's carrying a large knife. The other two boys are flanking him. The shortest one has sandy blonde hair and has a stocky build. The other is skinny with very short dark hair.

I start backing up, and Ash steps with me. They move at a steady pace to where we are standing. "Let's go," I whisper to Ash.

He nods and takes my hand. "You're right, let's go!" Ash yells and whips around.

The guy with the knife throws the knife and it just misses Ash's back and sticks into a nearby tree. I have no weapons, so I dodge for the knife that is stuck in the tree. As I tug on the knife to remove it from the trunk, I feel a sharp blow to my arm. The pain is excruciating and I drop my arm to my side and duck my head as I see his fist come towards my face.

His fist slams into the tree instead and he grabs his sore hand and tries to soothe it. I take this opportunity to grab the knife and wiggle it free from the tree trunk.

He grabs my leg and I lose balance before tumbling

to the ground. He tries to seize my hand that's holding the knife so I switch the knife from my right hand to my left hand and slice his good arm. I kick him until I break free from his grip.

Out of the corner of my eye, I see Ash fighting off the skinny dark hair boy. I turn around to find the stocky build boy right behind me. He grabs my arm and yanks the knife from my grip. He swings the blade toward my abdomen, and I jump back. I watch as he holds the knife in front of him moving it from side to side.

For a split second he is distracted by his friend on the ground. I use that to my advantage and kick the knife from his hand. We both leap for the knife and he reaches it first. He's about to stab me in the chest when all of a sudden Ash is there and he grabs the boy's arm and twists it back until I hear a crack. The boy drops the knife and he falls to his knees in pain.

As I watch Ash pounding this boy, I see the tall boy, who hit the tree with his fist, come up behind Ash. Before I could warn him, the boy knocks Ash to the ground. Ash isn't moving. I start to scoot backwards until I can get up to run.

I feel someone grab my wrists. I try to break free of his hold, but nothing works. While I'm busy trying to escape from his grip, the stocky boy grabs my legs. I squirm and struggle, but they lift me off the ground and start carrying me.

My eyes start to sting, and within seconds they weren't holding a helpless girl anymore. They watch me change into a werewolf. "Whoa!" the tall boy screams. I growl at them, and the stocky boy takes something out of his pocket—a tiny gun with a needle in it.

As I start to leap at them, the stocky boy aims and shoots a needle in my side. It paralyzes me instantly and I fall. My eyes get heavy, and I see Ash tackle the stocky boy to the ground. They wrestle around for a while until Ash eventually defeats him. My vision is blurry and I see an outline of Ash fighting the tall boy before I fade away.

I'm not sure how much time passed, before I wake in my human form. I feel groggy, but I'm aware that Ash is next to me smoothing my hair with his fingers. When my head starts to clear, I ask Ash what happened.

He sighs. "I'm not sure. I thought you might know," he says, rubbing his neck.

"Do you think this was a random attack?" I ask him.

"I don't know really. I don't know how they even found us," Ash replies.

I get up and walk over to the stocky guy. I grab him by his shirt. "Did someone send you to kill us?" I ask.

"Not exactly!" he wails in pain and tries to pull loose.

"What does that mean?" I bark.

He swallows hard. "We weren't suppose to kill you," he whispers with a shaky voice.

I slap him. "You better do better than that or I'll tear your head off!" I scream in his face.

He holds his hands up. "Okay, he wanted us to find out if your survival abilities improved! And he wanted to know if you and him were still close!" he points to Ash.

I let go of his shirt. "Well go tell him that I am fully committed to my promise and wouldn't think about backing out!" I yell.

He backs up and grabs his other friends, and they run away. I turn back to Ash and notice he's holding his side. "Did you crack a rib?" I ask.

"I'm not sure, Serena. I've never had a broken rib before," he says trying to make light of the situation. He wobbles a bit, and I put my arm around his waist for support.

"Yeah, you did. You need some help," I tell him, and we start walking. His arm is sweaty and heavy. I stop to let him rest before continuing.

Ash lies down in the leaves, and I feel a chill from the wind. "What now?" I ask him.

"I'm not sure. This is your world," he says and huffs. I roll my eyes.

I sit down next to him.

"I don't want you to leave me!" he protests.

I scoot closer to him and stare at his face. Deep brown eyes, dirty blonde hair, a few freckles on his nose, thick, well shaped eyebrows that are two shades darker than his hair, and cute dimples whenever he smiles.

I lean forward and touch my lips to his nose. He quickly moves his face up until we kiss. I watch him close his eyes; then I close mine. I don't know how, but my mouth gets dry even with Ash's right there. I wait a few more seconds until I push away.

Ash turns his head away from me. "What are you doing?" I ask him with a small laugh.

"Elle said that if I did anything stupid to slap me," he says and shuts his eyes.

I laugh and turn him around. "That won't be the stupidest thing you'll ever do," I whisper.

"Well you can smack me in advance," he jokes, and I playfully slap his cheek.

"Can we go back now?" I beg him.

His face turns puzzled. "Where?" he asks.

"Home," I say and pull him to his feet. It starts to rain.

I look up, and the drops fall onto my face, cover my hair, and soak my clothes. I see Ash isn't any drier than I am and smile. "What?" he asks me, trying not to sound tough.

"You're so freaking wet!" I say not even trying to hide my laughter. Ash continues with the fake tough-guy attitude, so I just play along.

"You think that's funny?" he says, and I can't help but laugh some more. I can tell Ash is trying his hardest not to laugh. "I'll show you something funny!" He pokes my side. I giggle, and he continues poking me. I roll over laughing, and Ash is stretched over me.

"I guess we're all wet," I say, trying to avoid an uncomfortable situation.

"Yeah, I guess you're right!" Ash says. Ash doesn't attempt to move so I gently shove him aside and stand up.

"I won't slap you unless you do something really stupid!" I tell him.

He wipes off fake sweat from his forehead and sighs. "I'm glad to hear that! Wait. Do you mean like really, super stupid?" he says and stands up.

"Maybe," I giggle. My teeth chatter, and he wraps his arms around me. "Ash, you're kind of choking me!" His grip loosens and I sit down. "I think you're healing!" I say and smile up at him.

I lie against a small maple tree and wait for Ash to join me. He looks around the woods to ensure nothing is out there. He lies down and puts his head in my lap. We watch the rain wash the leaves as darkness sets in. The moon is peeking through the clouds. I lay my head against the tree and fall asleep.

CHAPTER 12

Click, clank, chirp; click, clank, chirp. This pattern continues until I open my eyes to see what is making the racket. A robin and a woodpecker are on a branch; whenever I see two birds chirping in a pattern, I think they are talking to each other.

Ash is gone when I reach my hand over to wake him. I look behind the tree and see two feet being dragged across the ground into a bush. I follow them; avoiding broken branches and crunchy leaves so I don't alert them.

"I told you we should have checked her first!" I hear a man whisper to someone else.

Why can't I have some peace? I think to myself.

"Yeah, you should have checked her. This guy doesn't have any weapons with him! I hope the chick is empty handed," another voice whispers.

Good, only two, I think.

"Come on then! Let's go get her!" the first voice says. They start walking back, and I run back to the tree and pretend to be asleep.

"Look at that ring! What do you think it's worth?" one man shouts.

"Shut your face! Do you want to wake the entire town up, you moron?" the other man yells. They start fighting until they remember why they came here.

They come over to me and hold my hand up. "That's a nice ring!" one man whispers and starts to take it off my finger. I smack his hand and yell for Ash.

I grab his arm and pull it down and bite him as hard as I could. Ash stumbles out of the bush and looks around confused until he realizes that I'm being robbed.

The two men see Ash coming towards them and they take off running.

"Wow!" I say, out of breath after they are gone. "You are a really deep sleeper!" I tell him.

"I wasn't sleeping! They hit me over the head. Why us?" he asks, frustrated.

I think about it and can come up with only one reason. "I'm being tested for something and you're along for the ride," I say through gritted teeth.

Ash walks over to a tree and slams his head against it. "I shouldn't have followed you!" he shouts.

"What?" I ask him, totally lost on his words.

"Remember that morning, when I first met you in the woods? I followed you. I didn't trip either. I smeared dirt all over me so you couldn't see me. And I was nervous about talking to you, so that's what I would do every day—just sit and wait for you to come," he confesses and hits his head again.

What?! Before we met in the woods that day he was stalking me! Well I guess it doesn't matter now, but I wish

163

that he had kept that to himself. He tilts his head back to hit the tree again.

I stop his head and pull him away. "I don't care," I assure him.

"Really?" he asks. I nod, and some wet hair falls in my face. He brushes it away with one swift movement. He leans forward, and I put my hand on his face. "No, you were being stupid," I say.

"We can't stay here for much longer," I say to Ash with a hard voice. "We'll freeze to death."

"Fine, you're right. But when it gets warmer, we come back," he says and holds out his hand. I meet it and shake it.

"Okay, here on the first warm day," I agree, and we walk back to my house.

"Elle! Elle, we're home!" I call when we get inside. "Elle? Elle?!" I start to panic. I feel a lump in my throat and my stomach is in knots. My senses are screaming that something isn't right.

I start looking around for her—in the bathroom, in the kitchen, and in all of the bedrooms. Not there! Ash stops looking in the living room when I hit the wall with my fist. "Where do you think she is?" I ask.

"Maybe she went for a walk. She's around somewhere. Where else could she be?" Ash sees that his words are not comforting me and it's like he read my mind because we both run out the door and head to the woods.

I'm having flashbacks of my dreams. "Elle! Elle, can you hear me?" I shriek, hoping she can respond. No answer as we keep calling out to her. Then I hear a scream in the distance.

I take off in that direction and fall. I get up and brush myself off and continue to run. "Elle!" I scream.

Another scream follows. I see Elle lying on the ground covered in blood. Next I see another girl around the age of sixteen walking away and disappearing into the thick woods. I drop down next to Elle. I take her hand and hear her gasping for air. Blood drips from her mouth and body. I don't know what to do.

"Elle, I'm here. Serena is here. You don't have to worry," I comfort her and stroke her light brown hair. Her nose is bleeding really badly.

I tell her how much I love her and she's the best person I've ever known. I beg her to hold on, but I know she's not going to make it. We start crying together and I'm squeezing her hand as if trying to pump life into her. Her eyes close and I lay my head on her chest listening to her heart beat. I kiss her forehead. "You are the most important thing to me and always will be," I whisper to her.

She tries to tell me something, but all I can hear is her saying that she loves me. I gently place her head in my lap. One of my tears falls onto her face, and I wipe it off. Her heartbeat is slowing down. I outline her face over and over again until her chest stops moving.

I lift her to my chest and bury my face in her shoulder and cry. "Come back to me Elle!" I scream and press down on her chest continuously, even though I know it's useless. "Breathe! I can't lose you, Elle! Breathe!" I shout until I have no energy. I break down and sob uncontrollably for several minutes. Ash comes over and pulls me away from Elle.

He is crying also, but he can't look at her. "Help me,"

I whisper to him. He pulls me in for a hug, but my legs are weak and I fall to the ground next to her lifeless body.

"We loved her and she loved us. There isn't any more we can do. Serena, she's gone," he says and pulls me up again.

This time I'm able to stand. I can't stop looking down at my baby sister lying there. Did she suffer long before we arrived? Was she scared? I wrap my arms around Ash and hold him close. "I can't leave her here." I finally say. "Go get the blanket off her bed and bring a shovel so we can bury her."

Ash leaves me standing there alone with Elle. It's not long before he returns with the blanket and shovel. After he hands me the blanket he starts to dig a hole near a large pine tree. Her body is becoming stiff and her fingers and toes are turning black. I gently wrap her tiny body inside the blanket. Before I cover her face, I kiss her on the cheek and say goodbye. Together, Ash and I place her in the shallow grave and shovel the loose dirt back into the hole.

This moment feels like a dream. I think about that as we walk together in silence back to my house. My dreams seem real and my life seems like a dream.

Ash reaches in front of me and opens the door. We walk in, and I go to her room and open her closet door. The closet opens with a creak, and I pull out her long, white dress with a small bow in the front and bring it to Ash.

When he sees it, he starts crying again. "This," I say choking on my words, "was her favorite dress. She used to wear it everywhere until it got too small for her." I can't look at Ash without crying, so I focus on the dress.

"She didn't want to get rid of it because she loved it so much."

I start to feel anger building up inside me. I think about the girl we saw in the woods. Did she kill Elle? My eyes are drawn to the bow Elle bought me for my birthday. It's still in the corner where she put it.

Ash sees me walk towards the bow and shakes his head. It's too late; I'm on my way over to it and pick it up with my left hand. I switch it over to my right and pull its strings back.

"Serena, Elle is gone and you can't bring her back by killing someone. If you shoot that girl, *you'll* be a target," Ash tries to talk me out of it, but my mind is set. My new mission is to find that girl and make her pay for what she did to Elle.

"I don't care anymore, Ash. Elle is my little sister." I stop the tears, and anger flushes over my entire soul.

"Killing that girl is not going to make you feel better, Serena!" Ash starts, getting desperate.

"You're right Ash. It won't. Nothing ever will!" I say and head for the door. I pull the dress close to my face and take in its scent before I put the dress down on the couch. Ash catches my arm.

"Serena, please don't!" he pleads. I shoot a mean look at Ash, and he lets go of my arm. "Serena, you're going to make it worse than it already is," he whispers.

"Am I?" I challenge him.

"Yes, you are! What are you trying to accomplish?" Ash is trying to control his temper, but his face is turning red. I take one step backward and grip Ash's arms and slap him in the face. I'm sure he wasn't expecting that, but neither was I. He stands there looking at me with pity in his eyes. I shove him away and dart for the door.

The first place I set out to find this girl is the town square. I search everywhere from the bakery to the ice stand, and as soon as I'm about to give up, I see her. She's a tall brunette with black eyes that seem cold and dark. I knock an arrow and ease my way over to her slowly, observing her every move. She is alone and obviously waiting for someone. She looks my way, and her eyes widen with fear. She takes off running; I chase after her through the square and into an unfamiliar area of the woods.

She is fast, and I have a hard time catching up to her. I'm almost out of breath when she trips over a root and crawls backward. "Please don't kill me!" she screams and begs. I point the bow and aim it at her neck. "Elle wanted me to kill her!" she shrieks.

I lower my bow and give her a sharp look. "That's impossible. My sister loved life," I tell her.

"I'm telling you the truth. Elle told me to kill her, because she thought that someone else wanted her dead. She said that she didn't want you to worry about protecting her anymore," the girl says as she begins to cry.

I raise my bow. "Stop crying or this is going through your head!" I shout, and she shuts up. "If this is true, what's my name?" I ask her. If she knows my name, I'll let her go, because Elle would mention my name in her death wish.

The girl looks puzzled for a second. "Um, Anna?" she stammers. She made up the entire thing, but Elle must have given her some information.

"Time's up," I say as I release the string. The girl's eyes

widen. She screams as I aim the arrow at her in the throat. I hear her gurgle before everything is silent.

I have no sympathy for her. She murdered my innocent sister for no reason. I look at the girl. Blood seeps steadily from the neck wound. It went through the bottom of her neck and entered the ground before stopping. I kick her arm to make sure she's dead. I swear her eyes fluttered a bit, but I ignore it. I realize that I have never been in this part of the woods, so I decide to walk straight until I'm out. I turn my back on her and begin walking.

Ash was right. I don't feel any better after killing her.

"Nice try werewolf," I hear behind me. I spin around to find a half creature, half human girl with large fangs, red eyes, and scaly skin. I recognize it as the girl I just killed. "You're a demon just like Victoria! I thought I killed you!" I shriek and knock another arrow. I aim and shoot it at her chest, but it misses and hits her shoulder.

She screams an evil noise as she pulls the arrow from her shoulder and throws it back at me. I dodge it and begin to shoot more arrows at her. Only a handful hit her; the others miss by just a hair. She is changing quickly into a creature and less human. I begin to panic.

She lunges for me and knocks me onto the cold ground. An arrow is sticking out of her arm, and I pull it out and bury it into her stomach. She pulls it out and slaps me in the face with her sharp claws. Her voice is deep. "You're lucky I didn't kill *him* instead!" she snarls in my face.

"What?" I ask.

"You didn't think I knew about your little agreement, did you? Well your kind can kill us. Once the demons found out there was another pack of wolves they sent me out to find and kill them," she says, wrapping her long clawed fingers around my neck.

"Elle wasn't a werewolf! I am!" I scream at her.

I don't think about it. I just scream it as loud as I can. "Ash! Ash, help me! Ash!" I scream and kick.

"Shut up! He can't hear you!" she yells and scratches my neck barely missing my jaw. "I'm going to have fun making you suffer just like your little sister," she tells me. I feel my eyes beginning to change, and I feel a new tingling all over my body. Just as she is about to joke me I transform from human to werewolf. She jumps off me and opens her wings.

She barely gets two feet off the ground before I trap her wings in my powerful jaws and shake her back to the ground. I end up tearing most of her wing off and then I clamp down on her leg and fling her against a tree. I hear crunching sounds as the bones shatter within.

I leap for her face and tear at it with my sharp teeth. She shrieks and tries to pull me off her. I get off her and her limp body slides down the tree. The right side of her face is gushing blood.

I'm not sure if she's really dead this time, so I shove my paw into her chest until it comes out the other side. Her eyes roll to the back of her head. She exhales one last time. I start to feel some satisfaction for finishing her right the second time.

I turn back into my human form and run towards my house to find Ash. "Ash!" I scream. "Ash!" I scream again.

"Serena?" he calls back.

"Ash, you've got to come with me and see this!"

I scream to him. I turn back to the woods and start running. He follows me back into the woods and tries to catch up to me as I lead him back to the demon. I hear Ash breathing hard from the run and he comes up behind me.

I point to the demon. This is what killed Elle. It wasn't a werewolf. It was a demon. The demon was sent on a mission to kill the wolves and she thought Elle was a werewolf." I ramble.

He puts his arm around me and spins me away from the demon. He pulls me close to him and I can feel his warm breath in my face. I press my nose to his. "I did the right thing by going after it. That girl was a demon," I repeat. Ash shifts his head to look at the demon, but I grab his face and make him look at me.

"I worry about you Serena. You can't take on the bad guys by yourself. Maybe we should—"

I can tell he is out of breath, so I stop him. "I will fight for you. All I have now is you. Elle is gone, and so is Liam," I say and pull his face closer to mine. Ash tries to back up, but I lean in and touch his lips with mine.

I thought it was impossible, but each time we kiss it feels like the first time. I wonder if Liam can see us from heaven, if he is in heaven. Do wolves go to heaven? If so, did Liam get in? These thoughts fill my head, and I completely forget that Ash and I are kissing.

I pull away and put my head on his shoulder. "Can we go home?" I ask him.

"Let's go home," he says.

The sun is starting to set, and the night air is cool. He walks me to the door and I kiss his forehead. "You can go home now," I tell him.

He opens the door and walks in with me. "I know," he says as he shuts the door behind me.

The house is warmer but not by much. I hurry to my room to change out of these dirty clothes.

Ash stays outside my bedroom until I'm in my most comfortable pajamas. I open the door and pose for him. "Cute, Serena, very cute," he says sarcastically.

I drop my arms and frown. "You don't like them?" I ask and twirl again. My white tank top and fuzzy blue-and-green pants cling to me.

"I do. But a tank top? Won't you be cold?" he asks with a worried voice.

I stop and put my hands on my hips. "I'm not going to be cold. I have extra blankets to keep me warm," I whisper.

Ash leans close to my face. "Why are you whispering?" he mimics my voice, and I playfully push him away. He laughs and I walk back into my room Ash follows me. I crawl into my warm bed and pull the blankets over me. Ash sits down next to me.

"What are you still doing here?" I ask.

"What do you mean? Isn't this our home?" he asks.

"Fine," I say and close my eyes. I easily fall asleep, maybe it's because Ash is here with me and I feel safe for the first time. Whatever the reason is, I'm glad to have fallen asleep so fast. I need to escape the day.

CHAPTER 13

I shiver and pull the blankets over my shoulders. They pull back off; I grab them and yank them to my neck. They fall off again. I'm starting to get irritated; I pull them over my head and hang onto them. I feel a tug and resist.

"Kiwi! You up?" Ash's voice is loud. I push his face away and lazily open my eyes.

Now I am. Thanks a bunch for waking me!" I say and sit up.

"Great! I was wondering if you wanted to go for a morning walk." My eyes lock with his; his normal sweet face is twisted into a sad puppy dog expression. I can't help but smile at his lame attempt to get me to go on a walk this early.

"That doesn't work on me, you know," I grunt and stand on the cool floor.

"Please! It's nice out!" he argues and opens my window curtains. Frost covers every inch of it. He immediately shuts the curtains and smiles. He can be aggravating, but I love him.

"Okay fine!" I agree and shove him out the door.

"I'm getting ready, so stay out," I tell him and shut the door.

I'm moody this morning, because I'm up at four thirty. I put on my blue sweater and heavy dark jeans to coordinate with the dark colors outside. I grab my blue jacket that looks a lot like Ash's and pull it on. I go to my dresser and take out warm socks and slip them on.

Ash was leaning against the door as I open it. He struggles to regain his balance. "Aw, you're so cute! You're like a fluffy fish!" he exclaims and rubs his hand on my arm.

"A fish?" I ask him.

He shrugs. "Well, you're blue, and fish are always in water, and that's the only thing I could think of at the moment," he tells me. My mood lightens.

"Come on! Where do you want to go?" I say and tug on his arm like when Elle used to want something from me. I got up at four in the morning; so there better be a good reason you got me out of bed.

He looks up at the ceiling and exhales loudly. "Um, how about the pond?" he says with a smile. Is he insane?! It is freezing outside. Just thinking about how cold the water must be makes me shiver.

"We can't swim, but we can ice skate," he tells me and looks back down.

"No deal," I say and head back into my room.

Ash grabs my hand and twirls me around. "The ice is thick enough!" he protests.

"Ash, it's not safe!" I raise my voice slightly.

"Yes it is!" he says and pulls me away from the door. I try to walk backward, but he keeps on dragging me to the door. I sit down and cross my arms.

"I'm not moving," I huff and turn my head.

"Fine, I'll just carry you," Ash says and picks me up.

"What? Wait!" I shout. Too late, I'm already slung over his shoulder. He starts walking, and I pound my fists on his back. "Put me down! I don't want to go!" I shout. He ignores me and keeps on going.

I finally give up and roll my eyes. "You're impossible!" I huff. By now we are passing the square. I've gotten used to people staring, so when they glance over, I look away.

"I know," he whispers as a group of girls turn around. I see them whispering, and a short brunette calls Ash's name. He starts to turn, but I tell him that it's only some stupid girls trying to get his attention.

He continues walking and shifts me a little. I feel like I'm about to drop. "Ash, are you sure that I'm not going to fall?" I ask him.

"I'm positive," he assures me.

My hip shifts a bit, and I fall from his grasp. I land and roll over onto the frosty ground. "Yeah, you're positive that I'm not going to fall!" I gasp sarcastically. I turn onto my side, and my nose is literally an inch from someone's shoe. My eyes trail to the person's face.

"Hello," he says. He stretches his hand to help me up, but Ash pushes his hand out of the way. I grab onto Ash's hand and stand up. "Hey, remember me? I'm the guy who helped your friend," he reminds me.

How could I forget? He saved Liam's life. I'm glad he was walking through the woods at that time and helped Liam. I nod.

"Yeah, I remember you. I don't know how to tell you this, but Liam is dead," I say.

His smile quickly fades. "Oh, I'm sorry. Was it something that I did?" his face turns red.

I feel awful. "No, it's was nothing you did. It was my fault; I killed him," I admit. His face goes from depressed to shock.

"You what? How? Why?" he stumbles with his speech.

"He tried to harm—well, more like kill him." I point to Ash, and he waves. "And I was protecting him. Liam would have killed him if I didn't stop him." I think I told him too much and stop talking.

"Liam?" he asks, obviously puzzled.

"Yes," I tell him.

He seems to be taking the news well when he looks at me and smiles. "I would do the same if it was you and me," he says and puts his hand on my shoulder. He must have forgotten that Ash is standing right there, and Ash grinds his teeth.

"Sure," I mumble and brush his hand off.

"Why did he try to kill him?" he asks me.

"It's a long story. I don't want to talk about it," I say and stand next to Ash.

He shrugs. "Hey, since we ran into each other, can I finally have your name?"

I can't believe that he is asking me that in front of Ash. "Her name is Sarah Harten. Now get lost," Ash says and shoos him away.

When he is gone, I turn to Ash. "Why did you give him a fake name?" I ask.

"Because he was flirting with you. The last thing I want him to know is your name." He grabs my waist and twists me side to side.

"Jealous are ya?" I say with humor in my voice. We laugh and head to the pond.

We laugh and exchange stories while we walk.

"And Liam tripped over the rock and fell flat on his face!" I can barely say it without laughing. "That helped me take the lead by just a tad, and I won the race." We burst out laughing. "He was really sick that day and I ended up winning the race. If Liam wasn't sick, he would have won. He was the fastest runner in Pine Hill. It figures, after all he was a werewolf." We stop laughing.

"Okay, my turn. Let's see. Did I tell you the time I taught Drew how to swim?" he asks me. I shake my head, and he starts to tell his story. "Well I was seven, and he was five. It was summer time; this was also the first time I found our river. We woke up super early so we could get to school on time after the lesson, and when we got there, Drew said he didn't want to learn. I told him to at least try, so he did and almost drowned."

"I dragged him out of the water, and he tried to run away. I grabbed him and we jumped in. Naturally, he freaked and started kicking and splashing. It was hard to keep a good grip on him, and he slipped out of my hands. He was swept away by the current. I got out and started running downstream telling him to keep his head above water. I was able to save him but I don't think he ever forgave me for it." He looks at me and nudges my arm. I smile.

"We need to name it," I say.

"What?"

"You know, give it a name so we don't have to keep calling it Ash's river or the river we always go to," I tell him.

"Okay, what do you want to name it?" he asks.

I have to think about this for a while. I want it to be something meaningful but short. "I don't know. How about ESA River? The first letters of Elle, Serena and Ash."

His face lights up. "That is not a bad name, I like it." His voice cracks and he coughs.

"Finish your story," I urge him.

He points in front of him. "We are here!" he exclaims and runs ahead. I catch up to him and skid on some ice.

"Ouch! Careful, there's an ice patch over here!" I yell to him. He stops and bends down to brush the snow off the ice.

I try to stand up and slip again. "Ash, I don't think this is safe. I want to get off!" I call.

He swishes his hand in the air and tells me that it's perfectly safe. I trust him and slowly stand up. Ash makes his way over to me and grabs my wrist. My feet fumble for a minute, but I get the hang of it soon enough. In only a few minutes I'm able to stay up without falling. Ash is being silly and showing off his skating talents.

He skates over a hidden rock and takes a face-first head dive into a snow bank. "Hey, show off, smooth landing," I call to him. I can't help but smile at him.

I hear the ice crack under my feet. My smile fades, and I try to head for shore, but I slip onto my stomach. Ash pulls his head out of the snow, and is shaking it off.

"Ash! Ash!" I shriek. He stops and looks over at me. I drag myself a couple inches but am quickly consumed by the freezing water.

The first thought that runs through my mind is *I'm going to die*. I'm dragged under, and my hands struggle to find the hole I fell through to hold onto the edge. I pull myself up and try to call Ash's name again, but all that comes out is a pitiful choke and a high-pitched cry.

I hear more ice cracking and feel something grab my arms. I open my eyes and see two hands wrapped around my forearms. I quickly shut my eyes again, because the icy sting of the water is unbearable. I'm being dragged to the surface by Ash. He pulls me onto the snow covered ground, and I gasp for air. I shake uncontrollably from the bitter cold water.

My vision is blurry, and I can't stop my body from shaking. Ash removes my wet coat and wraps his coat around me. I can tell he's panicking, because I can hear heavy breathing and busy hands trying everything they can to get me warm. I can't really do anything other than pray that I don't die right here and now.

I feel Ash's arms wrapped tight around me, but I keep shaking. He must feel horrible right now, because he almost killed his fiancée. "Do you think it would help if I transform into a werewolf?" I ask

He looks at me and chuckles, "I don't think I can stand the smell of a wet dog."

"I think you need to back away and don't look at me when I transform. I hate that look!" I chatter jokingly. Ash backs away and turns his back to me. I concentrate and transform into a werewolf. I feel very warm and comfortable now. I look at Ash and he remains still with his back to me.

I switch back to human form and grab his coat and wrap it around me. It worked. I stop shaking. "You can look now. Did you think I was going to die?" I tease him. He frowns.

"Yes, you fell through ice into freezing cold water!" he says with a whiny voice.

"Oh," I say. I guess he really did think I was going to die. His cheeks and nose are red, and he looks at the ground. "Are you upset because you almost drowned me?" I tease. He nods. "Well don't be. I'm fine now," I tell him and wiggle my arms around him.

"How is it that I keep hurting you?" His voice is low.

I start to worry and put my hands on his cheeks. "My hair is out of my face," I say and move close to his face. He pushes me back. "Don't make me tangle my fingers in your hair again," I say and move my hands to the back of his head and entwine my fingers into his hair. I pull my head to his, and he turns his face away from me.

"I caused this Serena," he says.

"It wasn't your fault, Ash. You didn't know the ice was thin," I try to comfort him.

"It was my fault—all of it! I'm so stupid! I should have never—"

He doesn't finish, because I grab his face and kiss him. He tries to pull back, but I just lock my fingers in his hair and hold his face to mine. His hands find mine and peel my fingers off one by one.

He shoves me away. "Why are you blaming yourself? It wasn't your fault? It was only thin ice, Ash! You saved me and that should mean something," I say. He turns around and glares at me.

"What? You don't get it," he shouts at me.

"Yes I do get it. It's not your fault you were just trying to have fun," I argue.

He walks up to me; his face almost touches mine. "It's

more than what just happened in the pond. We seem to be in a constant nightmare and we can't wake up. This is our reality, and you need to get your head out of the clouds before you end up dead!" he yells and turns away.

I have mixed emotions after he finishes ranting. Tears run down my face, but I refuse to let him see how much that really hurt me. "Fine, if you really feel that way, I guess we should break it off," I say and walk away.

"What about the next werewolf, child, pup thing?" he asks, not turning around.

I hold my head up high when I state my fate. "They'll see that I have nothing to offer them, and they'll kill me. Don't worry. After that, you can find someone else to marry," I try to hurt him with words.

Ash turns and touches my shoulder. "Hey, I'm sorry," he whispers.

I shove his hand off me and start running. I begin to run home but remember that Elle isn't there to comfort me. I change direction and head to another place I find peace. I look up at the massive tree and swiftly climb its limbs and sit on a lofty branch.

I bury my head in my knees and start weeping. I'm surprised that I still have tears left from all of the other dreadful moments in my life. What is his problem? I know he apologized, but does he have to be such a jerk? Should I have just let him take all the blame for me falling through the ice?

My thoughts trail to his most hurtful words: *You need to get your head out of the clouds before you end up dead!* What did that mean? Does he mean that as long as he's around, I'll always get hurt, and I have to start facing that fact? Does he still want to be with me? Of course he does. He wouldn't want me dead; he cares too much to let me die. Lots of thoughts flood my head about what will become of me if I don't abide by the demands of the werewolves. Ash will be the only living soul that will ever know about the werewolf existence and the death it brought to the little town.

A stick cracks in the distance, and I raise my head above my knees. I expect it to be Ash, but it is an unexpected visit from the old werewolf. I don't want to talk, so I keep quiet and stay hidden inside the tree. He is human now; from my bird's-eye view it looks like he's diminutive.

"Serena. Beloved Serena, where are you?" he calls in a whisper. *'Beloved Serena!'* I silently imitate his voice, but in a higher more obnoxious tone. I sneer to myself, *Yeah right old man.*

He looks around, and by the expression on his face, I can tell he is starting to lose patience. "Serena, I know you're here. Come out. It's about ... uh, um, Cash or whatever his name is."

I don't buy it and cling to the tree. He gets irked by my silence and throws his hands in the air. "Fine, be that way! You know part of the deal was that we won't hurt him, but if you're being stubborn, I guess he'll have to take care of business. It's not like you can't find another boy," he taunts.

I grit my teeth so hard my gums hurt. "What do you want from me?" I shout.

He looks my way and smiles. "We're worried you're having second thoughts. I think we need to motivate you. If you scream, lover boy will come to your rescue and well–" he says and turns into a werewolf.

"What makes you think I'll–" He presses his giant

paws against the trunk. I hear a pop and cracking. "Wait! You can't kill me. You need me!" I yell. He continues to press against the tree. I hear more cracking and popping from below. I hold tightly to the branch. I feel a jolt, and the tree starts falling.

I cave. I scream for him to stop. I immediately cover my mouth, but I know that Ash would have heard it.

As I start to fall, my stomach gets butterflies inside of it, and a branch scrapes my left arm. About six feet before I hit the ground, the werewolf's jaws gently grab me from the branch and pull me out of the tree.

It falls with a thump and lies there, still and lifeless, like my sister, Liam, and my parents. He sets me down and looks around. Ash isn't here; go figure, since he's such a slow runner, but the werewolf doesn't know that. I scurry away and change into werewolf. I turn back around and head into the direction where Ash would be coming. I see him running towards me. I grab him and keep running away from the old werewolf.

"Serena, what's going on?" he demands and looks behind us. Apparently he spotted the other werewolf chasing us. "Run, Serena, and don't stop!" he shouts, and I speed up.

I wait until the werewolf is almost on my tail and make a sharp turn in front of a big tree. I turn in time, but he slams into it. He gives up after that and walks away with his head down, grunting and snorting angrily. I stop running and catch my breath. I drop Ash on the ground, transform back into human.

I lean my back against a large tree. I wipe beads of sweat from my forehead, pick some snow up, and cover my face in it. Ash's shirt is torn from where my claws went in it. "I'm sorry I ran away and almost got myself killed. See, it wasn't hard to admit that I nearly killed myself," I say and drop the snow.

"I'm sorry for getting in your face and yelling at you," Ash says sincerely and walks over to me. He brushes a strand of hair out of my face and leans forward. I stop him and back up. He looks confused. "You were the one who wanted to kiss me, remember? Our timing must be off," he says and leans forward yet again.

I close my eyes and step away. "Stop. You're right. I will end up dead if I don't snap back into reality," I tell him and turn away from him.

"I was mad, Serena! Don't listen to anything I say when I'm like that!" he raises his voice.

"It doesn't matter now. What's done is done. I'm going home," I tell him.

He runs up to me, and I start to take off, but he keeps a strong hold on my arms. I struggle to get away. I may be fast, but Ash is incredibly strong. I stop resisting for a second and turn around.

"Let go," I say as calmly emphasizing both words.

"What home Serena?" He barks at me. "You have no friends, no family to run to. That's what home is, friends and family." My mouth drops slightly open and my eyes start watering. Ash slowly looks away from me, knowing how much that hurt me.

I yank my arm free of his grasp and begin to run. When Ash calls for me. I turn around and face him. "Are we breaking up?" he asks, and his eyebrows raise.

"I don't know," is all I can manage to say before I start crying.

I sprint back to my house and lock myself in my room.

I turn my back on a wall and slide down it. "Ugh! How come everything in my life is so complicated?" I scream into my hands. I really hope Ash doesn't come in and try to make me feel better, even though a part of me wants him to.

I feel extremely emotional and I think about Elle and how much I miss her. The house is drafty and door creaks open a bit. I look up hoping it was Ash, but no one is there. My eye catches a single small blue glove under the bed. I reach for it and start to tear up. It belonged to Elle.

"Why me?" I whisper to the ceiling. "Why Elle? Why Liam? What did I *ever* do to deserve any of this?"

"Sometimes you don't do anything to deserve it. It just happens," Liam's voice comes from the doorway. I must be hearing things now. I look up with some weird hope that Liam would be standing there like he used to. My eyes trail the floor and up to his face—normal, average Liam is standing right in front of me.

I stand up quickly and brush the hair out of my eyes. "Liam? How is this possible? Are you a ghost? I have so much to tell you," I ramble. I want to wrap my arms around him, but I know I'm hallucinating.

"Serena, it's really me. I'm not a ghost, because I never really died. Werewolf healing abilities, remember?" he says and shrugs.

"That's not possible! I-I tore your face off! And, and you had a funeral and everything!" I scream and grab a pillow and squeeze it. None of this makes sense.

"Yeah, and it was challenging to scratch my way out of the coffin, but I managed before I starved to death! I had a nice-sized meal after I got out," he tells me. I almost throw up.

"So you aren't dead?" I ask cautiously.

He shakes his head. "Nope. Do you want to touch me to make sure?" He holds out his arm. "I missed you Serena. But I wanted to give you time to forgive me for all the mean things I did to you," he says.

I'm still in shock to see him standing there. I don't know what to say, so I tell him what he already knows. "Elle is dead. A demon killed her." His expression changes and he drops his head. "You should also know that Ash and I are still together." He looks back up and his expression changes from sad to surprise. "When the werewolves find out you're still alive, they'll kill Ash and force us to be together," I say.

He sits down next to me and whispers in my ear, "And that will suck for you, because werewolves live until they have been cut with a special blade—the one Ash happened to own before he gave it up for a stupid ring for you." He pulls his face away from mine and studies my face.

How does he know that?

He crosses his arms over his chest. "So, you will marry him but not me? And you'd start a half-blood line forever rather than continue the pure blood?" he questions.

"Yes, because I was never in love with you. I am in love with Ash, and that is how it will stay until I'm dead."

He smiles, and it worries me. "Or until *he's* dead. Now that the blade is lost, we are immortal. He was too stupid to know the power he held in his hand. Once the pack discovers he doesn't have the blade anymore, he will be dead," Liam says and stands up. I stand up next to him.

"Then I'll find the blade to make sure that doesn't happen," I say boldly and head for the door.

Liam gets in front of me and blocks my path. "No you won't, because I won't let you," he says.

I pause for a second. "I will kill myself before I marry you," I tell him and try to walk past him.

He shifts when I do and back again. "Liam, move. I see you haven't changed at all," I say and hear the front door open.

I push him, but he shoves me back. I land on the bed and hit my head on the wall. I rub the back of my head. "Did I mention that Elle is dead?" I add when he comes over to me.

"That's a tragedy, but there's nothing I can do," he says.

I don't know who he is anymore! He always loved Elle like a sister, now he could care less if she's alive or dead. I get ready to smack him, but he catches my arms and sets them stiffly to my sides. He presses his lips against mine, and I try to block him out; it doesn't work, and I start shoving him away. That doesn't work either.

I jerk my head and jump to my feet, and he follows me. Liam backs me against the wall. He plants both of his hands on the wall on either side of me; trapping me. Liam tries to kiss me again, but the door opens, and Ash walks in. I guess he doesn't know who is kissing me and runs over to him and starts hitting him.

Liam backs off me, and I have to catch my breath while Ash finally figures out its Liam.

"Liam … isn't … dead!" I breathlessly say to Ash. He looks at him and then me.

Liam smiles. "Long time no see ashtray," with that,

he smirks at Ash. Ash hits Liam in the face several times with his fist yelling at Liam and calling him shocking names I didn't even think he would use...ever! I don't break it up until blood is pouring out of Liam's nose and bottom lip.

"Ash, please stop! You don't understand what's going on." I plead and tug on his shirt. Ash stops, and Liam's face starts to clear up.

"Yes, Ash, that's no way to treat someone who comes back from the dead to take back what is rightfully mine," Liam says, and I shoot him a dirty look.

Ash looks like he's going to hit him again, but I grab his arm. "No. If it'll make you feel better, I told him that I'm in love you," I tell Ash.

Liam rolls his eyes. "I don't buy it! *You* know you love me, *I* know you love me, and *he* knows you love me! That's why he gets so protective of you when I'm around," he shouts behind Ash.

I don't try to stop Ash when he whips around and shoves him. "I get protective of her when you're around, because I know you're just waiting for me to give up on Serena. That's not going to happen wolf boy!" he yells and gets in Liam's face.

"You obviously don't trust her or you would let her have a nice reunion with her oldest friend!" Liam spits the words into Ash's face. And then adds, "Ashtray."

Ash clenches Liam's throat and shoves him against the wall where I was. "If you ever touch her again, I will rip your throat out!" he shouts into his face.

Liam pushes Ash off him. "Go ahead! You can't kill me! Not without your precious little knife you can't!" Liam yells at Ash.

This is where I step in and show Liam that he shouldn't push it; it'll just backfire. I walk up behind Ash and grip his shoulders. He looks back, and I kiss him on the cheek—right in front of Liam. I just wanted one simple kiss, but Ash goes overboard to put it in Liam's face. I know this will torment Liam and I pull away from Ash.

Liam claps, and I get confused. "Nice show, Serena. Very believable, but it's going to take a lot more than that to prove that you don't like me." He smiles when he's done. But past that smirk, I can tell that what I just did cut deep.

I cling to Ash's side. "Well is this proof enough for you? Ash and I are getting married in a week." I surprise myself and can't believe I just uttered those words.

Ash puts his arm around me. "Yep, one week." He leans close to my ear. "A week?! You couldn't have waited longer?"

I shush him and tell him to go along with it. But when I see Liam's face, I know I shouldn't have said that. He is turning red, and his body is getting stiff. I have known him long enough to know that it's his attack look.

I pull on Ash's arm. "Leave now. I will calm him down," I say, and Ash leaves the room. As soon as he shuts the door, Liam rushes over to me and grabs me and shakes me.

"One week?! You aren't even eighteen! How can you be so stupid? You know that I can top whatever he has to offer. God, Serena, you aren't even in love with him! You don't know what love feels like. I do, and all you have to do is find that feeling for me that I know you have."

I'm dizzy, and I my legs feel like jelly. Liam grabs me and sets me down gently.

"You don't hurt someone you love," I whisper. I know that Liam knows that Ash will walk in soon, and he pushes a chair in front of the door. Sure enough, I hear Ash pounding on the door and demanding to be let in. I know the chair won't hold very long, and so does Liam. He walks over to me and takes my face in his hands. "I want you to stop the wedding," he says desperately.

"I didn't ask you what you wanted," I sass back.

He leans forward to try and kiss me, and I head butt him. He lets me go and runs for the farthest part of my room. His nose is bleeding, and he looks up at me with rage in his eyes.

Liam walks toward me, and I close my eyes. Liam picks me up by my elbows and sets me up. I open my eyes and see Liam's fist fly straight for my face. It hits my cheekbone, and my face slightly cracks. I fall back and I see stars. I can hear Ash slamming into the door with his fists like mad.

"I know you love me, but why is it so hard for you to admit it?" he asks and pulls me close to him. He is cold, really cold, and I don't have enough strength to resist. I am trapped inside his arms.

The door finally breaks open, and Ash charges in. He pushes Liam away from me. "I told you to stay away from her!" Ash barks.

"Yeah, well I'm supposed to do a lot of things that I don't do," Liam says and narrows his eyes at Ash.

My cheek is starting to heal and I'm starting to get my strength back.

"Well you better do one thing right—stay away from our wedding." Ash stands protectively in front of me.

Liam sees that and tilts his head to the side. "Aw, isn't that sweet? The swimmer boy and the wolf girl—how cute," he says sarcastically and turns to walk out of the room.

Ash stops him, and Liam swings back around and pushes Ash's arm off him. I can tell that Liam has had enough of being pushed around by Ash and will do something stupid like punching him. Liam's face lightens, and he walks past Ash and grabs my hand. Oh my God. I can't believe that he won't stop!

He tilts his head and presses his lips to mine. I don't move, because I know that if I do, it will make matters worse. He grabs the back of my head before he breaks away. He walks out of the room with a grin on his face. I look at Ash.

"I don't know why Liam did that." I say, and he shrugs. "I don't know why he doesn't let me go. I don't know how many ways to tell him, I'm not in love with him," I say and rest my head on Ash's shoulder.

After about a minute, I get bored and fall on my bed. I sigh, and Ash flops next to me. "What's on your mind? Liam? Me? Elle?"

I'm glad he's comfortable enough to ask me about my thoughts instead of speculating. "Us and our wedding," I respond. "Is there anyone you want to invite? I don't have anyone except my two aunts. What do you think about holding the ceremony by ESA River?" I start panicking because it's now a week away.

"I was going to invite Drew and my mom. I think we should keep it small. I think ESA River is the perfect place to get married. You worry about what to wear and I'll take care of the rest," he says and sits up.

"Okay," I agree. "But one thing: We will be married in spirit only." He looks at the floor.

"What do you mean?" he asks.

"We'll be law breakers if we get married in a week. Remember, the law is that you must be eighteen to legally get married." I refresh his memory and stand up.

"Well, we can get married again when it's legal." Ash says with a smile. I nod and walk out of the room. Ash follows me into the hallway and walks next to me. "Hey, you okay? You seem sort of depressed," he says while we walk to the kitchen.

"Yeah, I am, because Liam is going to try his hardest to kill you and find that knife before next week," I tell him and open the fridge.

The fridge is bare. I slam it shut and run my hands through my hair. Ash touches my arm. "Wait. What knife?"

I let my hands fall to my side. "Your old knife—the one you traded for my ring. I forgot to tell you that Liam said the only way you can kill a werewolf is with that knife. Otherwise, as you just witnessed, they heal and come back to life. We need to find that knife." I stop talking but my mind is going a mile a minute.

"How is that possible?" he questions. "Your father is dead and your mother is dead." He reminds me

I shrug and sit on the counter. "I didn't use the knife to kill Liam, but I did to kill my father. If Liam is telling the truth, my mother maybe alive, because I didn't stab her with the knife. I wonder why she hasn't showed her face again if she's alive." It doesn't matter right now. What matters is that we get that knife back." I say.

We don't say anything for a while until Ash interrupts

the silence. "I feel like a fool. I had a knife that was powerful enough to kill a werewolf, and I traded it for a ring," he says jokingly.

I barely hear what he says, because I'm thinking about when Liam kissed me. I wonder if he just wants to be with me because it's a tradition or if he truly loves me. He can't love me or why would he treat me so bad? That's it. "I knew Liam didn't love me!" I shout. I didn't intend for anyone to hear that but me. I probably shouldn't have shouted it, but I was so relieved to figure that out.

"It took you that long to find out that Liam doesn't love you?" Ash asks me.

"Wait. You knew? Why didn't you tell me?" I demand.

He shrugs. "That's something you had to figure out on your own." He leans close to my ear. "But he really wants you, and for that to happen, I have to be gone. He doesn't hate me; he just hates that you love me," he whispers in my ear.

I don't respond to Ash. I can't figure out why it bothers me that Ash never loved me. I move my head away from Ash. "Why are we just sitting here?" I say agitated.

Ash smiles and his eyes widen. "I think I might have an idea where the knife is," he says smugly.

I jump to my feet and run over to him. "Where?" I ask excitedly.

"Fine, but I want something first," he says.

I roll my eyes. "Stop joking around," I say.

"No, not that. I want to know if you would marry Liam if I died." He stares at me waiting for a reaction.

I hold his face and kiss his nose. "Never," I assure him.

He smiles. "Okay, I'm pretty sure the knife is still with the butcher. I sold it to him for money to buy your ring. I didn't tell anyone who I sold the knife to. Let's just hope none of the werewolves wanted to buy a steak from that butcher." He winks.

"Nice. Let's just get there before anyone else does." I grab a jacket lying on the arm of a chair and put it on.

"Come on, Ash! Let's go! This is going to be our freedom ticket from werewolf terrorism." I walk out the door.

Of course, I'm a little ahead of him when we arrive at the butcher's. I walk inside, and the butcher greets me.

"Hey, remember that knife that Ash sold you?" I ask him. He nods. "I need it back for a little bit," I say.

He throws his hands in the air. "I'm so sorry. A young man just bought it from me. He said it was urgent that he needs it. I am sorry," he apologizes again. I walk out as Ash walks in.

"Where's the blade?" he asks looking at my hands. "With Liam He beat us to the punch," I say and keep walking.

"We'll just have to find him," Ash says and takes my hand and pulls me close to him.

"No, I'm going alone. He will expect us to be together, and he will try to kill you. He *will* kill you this time," I mumble.

Ash just chuckles and squeezes my hand. "Then I'll be the distraction. He'll be focused on trying to kill me and won't even notice you," he says.

I hang my head. "But I don't really want Liam to die. I just got him back, and I hope you don't take this the wrong way, but I've missed my best friend" I don't really know what his reaction will be, but I want to be honest.

"I thought I was your best friend," Ash complains.

"Oh please, Ash! We both know that I think of you as more than a friend. Liam is the one person who cares about me that's not related," I say and look up a flock of birds flying over.

Ash groans and rolls his eyes. "You don't have a clue about what all the guys say about you, do you?"

Before I can respond, I see Liam in the distance. I take off running towards him and leave Ash behind.

"Liam," I whisper under my breath. He turns and sees me. I can see the glint of the knife in his pocket and charge faster.

He stops and opens his arms. "Serena! How good to see you here!" he says cheerfully. I keep running for him and tackle him to the ground. He holds his hands up. "Whoa there. A little too excited, are we?" He smiles, and I slap him.

"Shut up, Liam! And wipe that grin off your face!" I yell at him.

People walking by don't offer to help when they see us wrestling on the ground. "Someone is not happy. Is it because I kissed you? Fine, I'm so incredibly sorry that you can't admit your feelings for me!"

He pushes me off him with no effort whatsoever. I fall onto the snow-covered ground but regain my standing position fast enough. I hear people whispering but can't make out what they are saying. "Give it to me, Liam. I know you have it."

He raises his eyebrows. "No, you're just going to kill me with it, so why would I do that?"

"I just got you back," I say. "Do you really think I would want to kill you again? You're my best friend, but understand that Ash is the one I'm in love with."

Ash pushes through the crowd and walks behind Liam. I know what he's doing, and I want it to work, but for that to happen, he would need to be fully distracted. He looks at me with pained eyes and nods slowly. I take in a deep breath and step forward.

"You're right. I do feel something else for you. You're right about everything, all right? I admit that I have feelings for you. I'll ditch Ash, okay?" I can barely get the words through my teeth that are grinding together.

He steps forward. "Now was that so hard? I've been waiting so long to hear that," he says and takes another step forward.

Ash is slowly creeping up on him; he extends his arm and grabs hold of the blade.

Liam whips around and catches his hand. "Sorry, but I'll be needing that," Liam says and tightens his grip on Ash's hand. I run over to them and pull them apart. I hit Liam in the face and look at Ash's hand.

"Sorry, but I'll be needing him." I mimic Liam's tone, and Ash and I rush out of there.

Liam isn't far behind us when we reach my house. We barely make it in the house and I slam the door. Liam screams and yells, demanding to be let in. Ash comes to the window next to the door and pounds on it.

"Hey, Liam, watch this." Ash says and pulls me close.

Believe me, I really wanted to kiss him, but I push him away. "Kissing me to make Liam mad will not solve anything!" I shout. I calm down and put a hand on Ash's arm.

"She won't even kiss you!" Liam yells from outside.

I bang on the door. "Shut up, Liam!" I shout and turn back to Ash. "I can reason with him; he won't kill me," I say.

"That's what you said last time, and you busted your cheek. Not to mention he kissed you twice."

"Three times," I mumble.

He pushes me back. "No, you aren't going out there by yourself," he says firmly.

I step forward and push him out of the doorframe. "I trust him, and I know what I'm doing. Please trust me." I try to reason with him.

"Fine, I'll be right here if you need anything—like prying him off you," Ash says.

I roll my eyes. "Let it go, Ash!" I laugh and walk outside. Liam stands there with his arms crossed looking at me.

He starts to speak, but I cut him off. "I told Ash that I would call him if you do anything stupid, so don't do anything stupid." I point at him.

He takes my finger in his hands. "No promises," is all he says before kissing my hand. I can't figure out why he pushes my buttons like he does.

"I warned you!" I say as I knock on the door and call for Ash. He comes out, his fists ready. "Man, what's with you? You can't be around her for five seconds before you—,"

I put my hand to his mouth. "Everyone needs to get along, okay? No need to make it worse," I say and drop my hand from his face. Without warning, Liam yanks me away from Ash and I lose my balance. Liam catches me before I fall.

I shove him away and step back from both of them. "Liam, can I please have the knife? I promise not to kill you." I ask nicely.

He smiles. "Sure, if you—" He pauses to think.

"Please don't make any demands," I tell him. He frowns and hands me the blade.

"There is one thing I forgot to tell you about that knife." His long pause makes me worry as I study the knife to make sure he didn't trick me. "When I discovered the power of that knife, I wanted to test it myself. I wanted to know if that knife could destroy a werewolf. I decided to conduct an experiment to test it. I waited and waited for the opportunity to steal the knife from Ash. Once I had the knife, I went looking for a werewolf. Obviously they aren't as common as you would think. Then there was you." He looks at me with a smile. "Of course, I'm joking."

Liam looks away from me when he speaks. "Then opportunity presented itself when your mom showed up. The fight between you and your mom in the woods didn't end quite the way you think it did. After you left your mother in the woods to die, I watched as her wounds started healing and knew she would go after you again. So I did you a favor and stopped her. Don't get me wrong; she was very excited to see me alive. She wrapped her arms around me and asked me to work with her to get you to."

He pauses and smiles. "You know- to follow werewolf traditions. It did break my heart, a little, when I hugged her back with the knife in my hand. I guess you can say my experiment worked."

There's a long silence after he confesses to killing my

mother. I'm not sure how to react to this news. A part of me wondered if my mom was still out there, but now I know she is gone forever. Shouldn't I feel relief it wasn't me who killed her? I should be mad at Liam but I can't be mad at him. I just got him back and I want to keep it that way.

Liam interrupts my thoughts. "No matter what you think about me right now, I do love you. I hope you will forgive me for all the bad I've caused, including trying to force myself on you," he says and walks away. That is the most unselfish thing I have ever heard Liam say.

I motion for Ash to go back inside, and he does reluctantly. "Liam!" I call for him.

He stops and walks back to me. "What?" he asks.

I don't know what to say or why I'm so emotional. He stares at me without taking advantage of the moment. I reach up and wrap my hands around his neck. I brush my lips against his. He doesn't move at first until he is sure it is what I want and then he presses his lips to mine. I move in closer to him and he wraps his arms around my waist. I'm surprised how right it feels.

He pulls away from me and I bend my head down and think about why I just did that. From the corner of my eye, I see Ash staring at us from the window. "I don't know what just happened, but I've got some explaining to do," I whisper maybe you should leave now. Liam tips my head up with his fingers and starts to kiss me again.

I back away and open the door leaving Liam standing there. Ash is sitting on the couch. He doesn't look up as I plop down next to him and put my arm around his shoulder.

"I'm sorry, but I had to do that. I had to convince

Liam that there was something between us to give us an advantage." I try to comfort him.

He looks at me. "We have the knife, isn't that enough?" He looks away from me and says, "I don't believe that kiss was part of a plan to trick him. Even I can see you have feelings for Liam." The outside of his eyes are red.

"What can I do to prove that I want you and only you?" I wait for his answer which doesn't come. "I can't believe you don't trust me. That's just great!" I say.

What Ash does next takes me by surprise. He pushes me back and falls on top of me and kisses me.

I try to sit up, but his right hand wraps around my head, and the left hand is holding my neck. This is really awkward for me, but Ash doesn't seem to notice. I break away.

"I don't know what you're thinking, but don't ever do that again," I say.

He leans away from me. "I'm sorry Serena," he says.

I look at the clock. "It's late," I mutter.

"I think we both need some sleep," Ash says and stands up.

I point to him. "Stay at your own house tonight, okay?" I say.

He laughs slightly and lies down on the couch. "I'll be right here when you wake up tomorrow," Ash tells me and closes his eyes. I head to my room and slam the door. I don't bother pulling the covers back, I just collapse on bed and fall asleep within minutes.

I'm awakened in the middle of the night by a strange noise. I get out of bed, and notice my room looks different. I open my door slowly and look around the dark room. I don't hear anything, so I walk over to the couch and it's empty. The noise must have been the door shutting when Ash left. I open the door to see if I can convince him to come back, but when I open the door there is no one around. The moon is hidden by clouds and there is only blackness.

Just before I shut the door, I hear someone call my name. It sounds like Elle is calling me. My heart starts racing and I call to her. I can't see anything because it's so dark outside. Something runs in front of me, but I can't make out what it is.

I call Elle's name again but this time louder. I walk cautiously forward into the darkness hoping to find Elle. As I approach the edge of the woods, I see a little girl running away from me. I start to chase her through the thick woods, but she stays ahead of me. I keep reaching out to grab her, but she disappears and then reappears in a different spot.

I see something run in front of me again but I can't figure out what it is. I hear Elle call my name again and my attention is back to finding the girl. A part of me wonders if Elle is playing a game, but I'm wary because I know my little sister can't be alive. Still there is that little bit of hope.

I'm startled and jump back when a little girl who sort of looks like Elle pops out from behind a tree. It's not my beautiful Elle. This girl has large fangs and she smile is extremely wide. Her eyes are beady, red and scary. Her voice is deep when she speaks to me, "Why didn't you protect me Serena?" And then she disappears into thin air.

"Wake up!" I hear someone shouting. I open my eyes and see Liam staring down at me. I look around and see I'm in the woods.

"How did I get here?" I ask. He looks at me and then away. That's when I noticed we weren't alone. Ash was standing nearby holding the knife.

"Serena, why were you in the woods?" Ash asks.

"I must have been walking in my sleep. Where's Elle?" I ask Liam. Liam and Ash both stare at me and don't say anything. "I know this sounds crazy, but Elle was calling me," I say.

"Elle is gone. You must have been dreaming." Ash says.

"It seemed so real." I shiver. "I'm so cold," I say and stand up. "How did you know where to find me?" I ask Liam.

"When I arrived at your house this morning, your door was wide open and no one was home," he sighs. My eyes bulge with surprise. "At first I thought you and Ash went somewhere, but when Ash showed up a few minutes later and didn't know you were missing, I took off to find you." He offers to put his arm around me, but I shake my head no and back up.

Ash pipes in and says, "I wanted to apologize for my behavior, but found *him* instead." He tries to conceal the knife behind his back.

I conclude that I must have been sleepwalking. Lucky for me I didn't undress last night or I would have frozen to death. "I miss Elle so much Liam," He wraps his coat around my arms and holds me close to warm me up. At least that's what I tell myself. "Thank you very much for saving my life, Liam."

He smiles. "I did save your life," he says and holds up his hands. He holds up one finger and boasts to Ash. "Point, Liam!" so Ash can hear him.

Ash rolls his eyes. "You're still many points behind, my friend—many, many points," Ash tells him. Liam shoots him a mean look but stops.

I didn't think it would take long before the bickering would start. At least I had a few minutes of peace with the three of us together.

"Not today Liam, I'm not in the mood," I say. I look at Ash. "And what time did you leave last night after we went to bed?" I regret the words as soon as they came out of my mouth.

I'm sure Liam wasn't happy to find out that Ash spent most of the night at my house. I look at Liam and see him leap forward onto Ash knocking him to the ground. Ash struggles to get up, and I try to peal Liam off of him. Ash's face goes white, and his lips turn a pale purple.

Liam is choking Ash. "Liam, get off! You're hurting him!" I yell yanking on his arm. He snarls at Ash and releases him.

Ash is gasping for air, and I look at Liam like I can't believe he just did that. "Why did you do that?" I ask him.

He shrugs. "I can't believe you just asked me that," he answers and motions to Ash who is still trying to take in as much oxygen as he can. "After what happened with us last night, you ask me why I want to kill this low life." With that said, he stuffs his hands in his pockets almost as if he were trying to restrain himself.

"Nothing happened. And I wish you would stop trying to kill him! Why are you so overly protective? Nothing's going to happen to me," I tell him.

He opens his mouth to speak, but I stop him. "The only thing you need to protect me from are those freaking werewolves." I try to calm down. "Ash is not going to hurt me," I tell him and sit down.

Ash is breathing fine now and gets up.

"Do I need to remind you he has the knife? He has it tucked under his jacket right now. If anything, *I'm* in danger." Liam points to Ash and then me. "This just isn't right." He walks a few steps and then stops. Without turning around he says, "You know just as well as I do we should be together," and continues walking away until he is out of sight.

"I swear someday I'm going to!" Ash starts but looks at me. "Never mind," he says and comes closer to me. I put my head on his shoulder. "Don't worry. Liam is all bark and no bite," I chuckle.

He rubs his neck and smiles. "Some bark," he says.

I feel the need to say something else, so I tell him about the dream.

"I really thought Elle was calling for me," I tell him.

"I think you miss her and your mind played tricks on you and that's why you ended up here." He puts his arm around me. "Let's go home." He says. I look up at him and slip out from under his arm. Ash looks puzzled. "What's wrong, Serena?" his voice is kind and soft.

"I think Liam might still be watching us." I whisper to him softly. Ash looks around and slowly lowers his gaze to me. Ash starts to shout out something and I cup my hand over his mouth.

"Please don't make this worse than it already is," I plead. He removes my hand from his mouth and looks at me. "Liam is upset about..." I pause. "He's worried about..." I shake my head. "Forget it. It's not like what I say matters anyways." Ash bends his head close to mine. I continue to look away.

"Maybe I can make all our troubles disappear..." he holds the knife up, the blade reflects the sun. I touch his arm.

"No, Ash. I couldn't ask anyone to kill him." A lump gathers in my throat. "No matter what he does."

Ash backs away from me. "There must be some exception to that. What if..." Ash stutters. "Maybe if he..." Ash has nothing. He grabs my arm and reflexively, I flinch. "Promise me that if he does anything like," But Ash is cut off by Liam's voice

"Like what ashtray?" Liam steps out from behind a large tree. He nods his head at me. "Do you really believe I would purposely hurt my dear Serena? I want to share my life with her and," before Liam is finished speaking, Ash is walking toward Liam. I catch up to Ash, tugging on his arm.

"Do you really think killing is the answer?" I shout in his face.

Ash whips around. "Says the girl who murders for revenge." Ash quickly shuts his mouth and squeezes his eyes shut knowing he said something wrong.

"So suddenly Elle is nothing?" I shout at him.

His face turns red and tries to tell me something else but I don't listen.

"Because last time I checked Elle was like a little sister to you. She actually *was* your little sister since you became my fiancé!"

"Serena, I didn't mean it like that." he tells me. "Of course Elle was my little sister, but..." he stops there. I glance at Liam who is watching us and amusement sweeps his face.

"But what Ash?" I shout. Ash's face turns bright red not only from me yelling at him, but from the embarrassment of being yelled at in front of Liam.

"I don't know." He responds.

Liam comes to my side, putting his arm around my waist. Ash reaches for my arm, but I pull back. "You struck out ashtray." Liam quietly tells him.

Ash desperately searches my face for a response. I shake my head slightly. "I'm sorry, Ash. Let's both cool down and spend some time away from each other. Okay?" I say slowly.

His eyes grow hard and through grinding teeth, he says, "Sure, whatever."

I mouth the words thank you and let Liam turn me around with his arm still around my waist and begin walking in the opposite direction.

"Tell your wolf friends I'm right here if they still want to kill me." Ash spouts off. I turn my head to find Ash on his knees staring back at me. My eyes sting as tears start to fall.

Liam lowers his mouth to my ear. "Sore loser," he says, "Just kidding."

We walk back to my house without saying anything. I sit on the couch and Liam goes to the kitchen to find something to eat. He brings out some bread and cheese and hands it to me. I eat it quickly not realizing how hungry I was until now. My aunt must have stopped by and brought some food. "Liam." He looks down at me and smiles.

"What?"

When I don't respond, Liam tilts my chin up. My back stiffens. He closes his eyes and presses his lips to mine. I can't stop thinking of Ash. What if something bad happened to Ash? What if Ash is dead? Or getting ripped apart by a demon? My face grows hot. I pull away and sit up.

"This is wrong." I tell Liam.

"I would disagree. You always knew it was me you'd end up with."

I shake my head. "I'm sorry, but I've got to go find Ash and make sure he's okay." I stand up. Liam grabs my wrist.

"Don't Serena. Please." He says.

"I'm sorry." I say and free my hand from Liam. It doesn't matter anyway because he reaches up and grabs my elbow while standing up.

"Stay," his voice scares me. "Please." Not knowing what I'm doing, I sit back down on the couch. Liam takes a seat next to me and buries his face in my hair. "I just don't want to lose you." Liam whispers in my ear.

I jump to my feet and run for the front door. I open the door and run out to find Ash. Liam doesn't bother following me.

"Ash." I call half-heartedly. "Ash." I wait several minutes for a response. I sit on the cool ground with my knees against my chest. I try one last time, "Ash, I need to know you're okay." My voice is weak and hardly makes a sound.

"Let me guess," Ash's voice makes me jump. I look up and he is leaning against a tree, the knife secure in his tight grip. "You didn't know what you were doing and what was happening until Liam said or did something to upset you." Ash pauses and sticks the knife in the side of the tree. "Now you want everything to be fine with us."

Shock floods over me. I nod.

"Well, things don't always end up the way we want," Ash takes a few steps closer to me. I'm frozen in place by his words. He walks slowly to me and bends down in front of me. "You, Serena, of all people should know how that feels."

"You're not making any sense." I whisper and move back a bit.

Ash follows me. "I don't know you anymore Serena," his breath has a different odor to it.

I blink rapidly to hold the tears back. Quietly I say, "This isn't you."

Ash lightly pushes my shoulder back. "Then who…" he stops in mid-sentence. He slides his hand into mine and holds it up. The ring sparkles as he slowly moves my hand back and forth. A sudden expression flows over his face and he gently puts my hand down to my side. Ash looks even more confused than me. He looks down at the ring he had given me not even a year ago after I turned sixteen. His eyes widen the same time his mouth drops slightly open. I back away from him. Ash looks at me with a blank expression on his face. Without warning, Ash slaps himself in the face…hard. I watch as Ash shakes his head from side to side.

I back away from him. "I don't know what you're doing, and I don't know why you're acting like this, but just stay away from me until you figure out what's wrong with you." I say and turn.

"Serena, wait!" Ash calls from behind me. His desperate pleads remind me of Liam when we fight. As soon as I'm a ways away from Ash I softly begin to cry.

I need to find out more about why my life is screwed

up and the only one who I can ask is Liam. I head to his house to get the answers. I walk up to Liam's back door and notice it is wide open. I invite myself inside. Not even two steps inside; I see a small glob of red/brown liquid on the floor. I bend down and dip my finger in it. I raise the sticky liquid to my nose. "Hey!" I look up and see Liam's father standing above me.

"Hello. Um, is Liam here?" I ask. He points to the couch. Sure enough, Liam is sitting on the couch looking down at his shoes smiling. He sees me and stands up. I throw myself into his arms and start crying. "My God, Serena, what happened?" he asks me.

"I don't know! Ash was acting strange and was not acting like himself." I say leaving his arms. Liam pulls me back in, but not before I could see a devious grin spread across his lips.

"I'm not going to say I told you so, Serena." Liam's hold tightens.

"Thanks Liam, I knew you'd make me feel better about it."

"Told you so!" he says and releases me.

I teasingly push him back and smile. "I told you so!" I imitate his voice.

"Told you so!" he repeats and picks me up and spins me around.

Liam and I go back and forth with the 'I told you so' thing for a while until his father interrupts us. "It's nice to see you two getting along." He walks by us grinning. I look back at Liam. He is smiling at me. I hit his forehead with the bottom of my hand.

"Don't act like getting on my good side is a big accomplishment." I tell him walking over to the couch and sitting. Liam sits next to me. I stop smiling for a moment and look at Liam. "I know I can't control what you think or your actions, but-" I can't find the right words after that. I lean forward to kiss Liam but then stop myself.

"This feels right with you here." Liam says and he gently kisses me. I don't tense up when he touches me this time. Instead I feel a warm sensation throughout my body as his lips make their way from my mouth to my neck.

"I never knew I could feel this way around you." I say and rest my head on his shoulder.

"How?" he asks.

"Please don't make me explain it." I pull away and look at him. "Liam, can I ask you something?" I sit back against the arm of the couch.

He puts his arm around the back of the couch. "Sure, what is it?"

"How did we become werewolves?" I inquire.

He looks confused. "Serena, I think you know how." His eyebrows dance up and down.

I playfully slap him on the shoulder. "Not *that* way Liam. How did werewolves come into existence?"

Liam takes in a deep breath and closes his eyes. "I'll tell you what I heard about our kind as told to me by my parents. Centuries ago, the Devil had a plan to create chaos and destroy the human race as we know it. He decided to create a team of creatures to help him carry out this plan. The Devil used his most despicable souls and turned them into demons. He gave them the ability to transform into humans." Liam stops and looks.

"Next, the Devil convinced a small group of humans that they could live forever if they agreed to be turned into werewolves. The devil was ready to carry out the plan and send the creatures into the world to start the mission. Shortly after they start creating havoc on the world there was tension among the two groups. One of the werewolves overhead one of the demons boasting about being second in command of the world once the mission was completed. For days the werewolves and demons were in a dispute about the high honored position."

"Finally the devil stepped in and said the demons' were to be second in command, for they had no souls and no love, nor compassion. But the werewolves on the other hand, did possess those traits, since they were made from humans," Liam clears his throat. "Well, some of us are more evil than others. After the Devil sided with the demons', the werewolves broke away from the Devil and ran off into the world to try and live among humans."

"The Devil was furious and so were the demons'. Without the werewolves, they could not carry out the plan. The devil made the mistake of giving the werewolves the ability to live forever. The Devil created a powerful weapon called the Dagger of Death to destroy the werewolves. The Devil gave the Dagger of Death to Diabo the demon. His mission was to locate and destroy all the werewolves. The Devil knew the only way to kill us was with the Dagger of Death."

I interrupt in the middle of the story. "Then how did Ash end up with the knife?"

Liam holds a finger to my lips. "Shh! Let me finish the story. Anyway, the demon sets out to destroy the werewolves. Diabo was able to destroy a few werewolves, but when it was discovered that the knife was the reason the werewolves were destroyed, the werewolves set a trap for Diabo. The werewolves destroyed Diabo, and hid the Dagger of Death so that it would never be found to destroy our kind again." Liam sucks in a deep breath. Now the demons are in a race to find the Dagger of Death. The Devil has told them that whoever finds the Dagger of Death will become second in command."

He pauses while I take in this information. "The Dagger of Death never surfaced until Ash came along." Liam sounds accusatory.

"Where do you think Ash found the knife?" I ask.

Liam shrugs and moves his head close to mine. "You don't think Ash might be a demon? Do you, Serena?" He moves his whole body closer to me so we're inches apart. "Has he ever given you reasons to believe he might not be who he says he is?" Liam asks.

"Do you think Victoria knew Ash had the knife? It seems like the demons have been around Pine Hill a lot lately." Liam skims his hand over mine onto my wrist and slips his hand into mine. I'm not sure what to believe. Liam twists my engagement ring off my finger. I stop him for a second, but let him take it off and set it on the table next to the couch.

"I don't know what to think," I say weakly and lean on Liam's arm. I close my eyes and feel Liam's warm breath over my face.

Liam's voice grows creepy. "You never know, he might just be." I try to ignore his last comment.

In my dreams tonight, Ash transforms into a demon. He kills Elle and then Liam. At the end, Ash comes for me.

I wake with a start. Sitting upright I must have fallen

asleep on Liam's couch. Liam is fast asleep on the floor and quietly snoring. It's dark in the house and I carefully step over Liam and walk towards the kitchen. I'm about to get a drink of water when I hear someone clear their throat. I turn and Ash is standing there. "I don't know what I did to make you mad at me, but I thought I'd be the one to say sorry first," he whispers. His eyes fall to my hand.

"Where is your ring?" he asks. I point to the table next to the couch. It lies there, small and elegant.

"Over there. And you know very well how you acted yesterday," I whisper.

He moves closer to me and I step back. Ash doesn't see Liam on the sleeping on the floor. I open the back door and motion for Ash to leave. He doesn't say anything and walks out. Liam's eyes flutter open as soon as I quietly shut the door.

"What was that?" Liam asks groggily.

"Nothing, I thought I heard something outside. It's early. Go back to sleep," I continue to whisper. He shrugs and lies back down, as soon as I'm sure he's asleep, I gently pick the ring up and slide it on and leave.

I run into Ash standing outside. He grabs me and we fall into the snow. "You just can't stay away from me." His voice is soft. I get up and shove him further into the snow.

"Oh please, like I would want anything to do with you after yesterday!" I say.

He stands up and brushes the snow off of himself. "What did I do to make you so mad? What happened yesterday? I don't remember; its hazy." he says.

I think about this for a minute and wonder if Ash

is telling the truth. "Ash I don't know who you are anymore." I say.

"I don't understand, Serena. Last time I checked I was your fiancée. So would you mind telling me what changed that?" he says.

"Where did you get the knife that kills the werewolves?" I ask.

"I found this knife one day when I was teaching some kids how to swim. I was underwater near the rocks edge when something shiny caught my eye. I found the knife wedged between two large rocks and it took me a few dives to retrieve it. It looked like a knife that was crafted from another time period. I found it strange that the blades were still sharp. Why is this important?" He says loudly.

I cover his mouth, but it's too late. I see a window open, and Liam's father's head pops out of it. His face turns red, and he calls for Liam. I don't have time to sort through this so I tell Ash to run.

He takes off, and I stagger behind. Liam runs out of the door and sees me.

"Why are you running off?" He sounds concerned for a brief second before he catches a glimpse of Ash running away.

"Don't, Liam. Please don't," I plead.

He ignores me and runs after Ash. I try to stop Liam by jumping in front of him. He trips over me and we both hit the ground hard. I expect him to keep running after Ash, but instead he holds me down. I try to kick, but he has me in a tight hold.

I see Ash coming back for me. I scream for him to go and that'll be fine, but he won't listen. A neighbor opens her window and screams at us. We all look in that direction. I feel Liam's grip loosen, and I punch his stomach. He releases me, and I stand up. Ash grabs my arm and we take off running. Liam isn't far behind, that is until Ash stumbles and falls.

Liam leaps towards Ash pinning him to the ground. Ash manages to get to his feet and I put myself in the middle of them, holding my hands against each of their chests.

Ash steps forward, and I scream at him to back off. He backs away, and we stand like this for the next minute. Liam walks forward. I scream, but he continues to walk. I scream louder; he pauses and then keeps on coming. The neighbor comes out of her house with a broom waving it at the boys. It's an elderly woman with snow-white hair and peach-colored lips. "Stay away from her! I'll hit you with this!" she shouts and waves the broom in the air.

Liam picks me up, and I scream for real. The woman comes after us with the broom and hits Liam many times until he finally lets me down. Ash comes to take me away, and she hits him with the broom as well.

She waves it in their faces, and they back off. She lowers the broom and reaches her hand to me. "Come, dear. You must be terrified." Her voice is kind and sweet.

I try to convince her to go back into her house. "I really appreciate your help, but these two are just playing around and it got a little rough."

She shakes her broom in the air as a warning to both of them and goes back into her house.

"I'm confused Serena. Are you in love with me or him?" Liam asks.

I run my fingers through my hair. "I'm not sure

anymore." I say, and Liam's face lights up. Ash's face loses color at the reaction of Liam.

I go home and lie down on the couch. "What have I done?" I ask myself. For the rest of the day, I stare at the wall thinking about how excited Liam must be to have a chance to be with me. I think of Ash and how I might have doomed our relationship forever. If I choose Liam, will Ash ever forgive me? Maybe, if I'm lucky. I glance at the clock.

"How is it already three o' clock?" I ask myself. I get up and grab my bow. "Might as well go hunting since there is nothing to do," I mumble to myself.

I head out to the woods and spend hours without seeing any game worth shooting. A couple of red squirrels and chipmunks tease me with their lack of size and meat. After I'm about to give up and head home, I spot a large buck wondering by. I aim, but not fully focused, I miss and the animal runs off. I kick myself for missing it. I come back to my empty little house, disappointingly empty handed and lean my bow against a wall.

I lie across my bed and daydream about Elle and all the things she could have done if she were still alive. I hear her laughter and remember her smiles. The little giggle she would let slip between her lips when she was embarrassed. I think about her getting married someday and having children. Then I start to think about my future and remember that my own daughter's life is mapped out for her before she is even born.

My stomach growls and I look for something to eat. I cook up some eggs and potatoes. It is now seven thirty, and I'm restless and full.

I look around and the house is a mess. I decide this

would be a good time to do chores around the house to take my mind off Liam and Ash. I take a pot outside and fill it to the brim with snow. I pack it in and fill it up some more. I take it back inside and set it over the stove, I light the fire and wait for the snow to melt. I walk back over to it and see the pot is a quarter of the way full with water.

I pour the water in a large tub and some soap. Next I throw in my dirty clothes. I let the clothes sit in the water and soak. I need more water so I bring the pot outside and fill it with snow again and bring it inside and boil it. I use this water to help wash the dishes and wash the table and the floors. After that, I just tidy everything up as much as possible and hang my clothes to dry. It's late and I can't keep my eyes open. I head to my bedroom and fall asleep.

My eyes open, and the world seems peaceful and calm this morning. I look around and admire my hard work from last night. Everything is picked up and clean. I think about the werewolf story that Liam told me yesterday and try to make sense of it. I need to get that knife away from Ash. It puts him in danger with both the werewolves and the demons. I sit up and stretch.

"Morning, Sunshine!" I hear Ash say entering my bedroom. I look at the foot of the bed, and he is waving at me. I pull the covers up to my neck even though I'm fully dressed.

"Don't you knock before coming into someone's bedroom?" I ask him.

"Sorry about that," he says and sits next to me.

"So what do you want to do today?" he asks as he tickles my feet through the covers.

I fling my legs over the other edge of the bed and sit up. "And why would I want to do something with you today?" I ask him. He frowns.

"Because you love me with all your heart..." Ash says and smiles wide.

I look at the floor. "I do love you, but I'm not sure how much." I say.

"You can't possibly mean that," he says. I look up at him. "After everything I did to be with you. My family is beginning to worry that there might be something wrong with me. Drew is having a tough time without his older brother being around. And you, Serena, have given up so much as well for us to be together." He moves closer.

It takes me several minutes to respond. "I need that knife back," and hold out my hand.

Ash walks over to me and sits next to me. "What?" He stares at me for awhile before continuing. "That knife is saving us from an untimely death." Ash puts his hand on mine. "But I'm happy to give it to you if that means we will be together."

I turn my head to look at him. "I can't make any promises right now." I tell him.

"What does that mean?" he asks and takes his hand from mine.

I look at him but don't respond. "I need to go to my house and get the knife." He says. "Do you want to go with me?"

"Is the knife somewhere safe? I ask.

"Yes, of course. I didn't bring it with me because I

thought Liam had a change of heart and doesn't plan to kill me anymore!" I chuckle

"It's not just Liam you need to protect yourself from. I need to warn you about the demons. Is it possible Victoria knew you had the Dagger of Death?" I ask.

"The what?" he asks.

"The knife. Liam told me about the knife's history and purpose. It belongs to the demons." The demons call the knife Dagger of Death." I hesitate to see if he's keeping up with me. "The demons use the knife to kill the werewolves. It's their mission."

"Let me see if I have this right. The demons are on a mission to kill the werewolves. You're a werewolf, so it seems that you're the one in danger and not me." He says seriously.

"You are in danger Ash. The demons are searching for the Dagger of Death, I mean knife. If they figure out you have it, they will kill you and anyone that gets in their way." I say. "I think that's why that demon killed Elle, I think that demon girl thought Elle had the knife or at least knew who had it."

"Why is the knife the only thing that can kill a werewolf?" He asks.

"The Devil created the werewolves so that they couldn't be destroyed. In essence, he granted them eternal life. When the werewolves defected from a plan to destroy mankind, the Devil created the Dagger of Death which was the only thing that could terminate the werewolf." I explain. "He gave the Dagger of Death to a demon and the demon was supposed to kill the werewolves, but the werewolves were able to outsmart the demon and they hid the Dagger of Death so that it could never be used to destroy another werewolf. The demons have been searching for it for centuries."

"In the meantime the werewolf population has increased, making it more difficult to wipe out the entire species." He concludes.

"It's called survival. The werewolves are making sure they keep producing generations to make it impossible for the demons to kill all the werewolves even if they find the Dagger of Death." That's why they wanted me and Liam to be together. There's a better chance at saving our species if werewolves stay within our own kind. If we have relationships with humans, the population of werewolves diminishes."

"So you're trying to decide if you love me enough to risk this reduction in population." He says with a grin.

"Yes, I guess you could say that." I say.

"It makes me feel better knowing you have a responsibility to do something good rather than just leaving me because you love someone else." He sighs.

"There's more." I pause. "It's not just saving the werewolf species that is causing me to not be with you." I say.

"Let me guess. You're falling in love with Liam." He looks devastated at this discovery.

"I can't deny my feelings for Liam. We have been friends for a long time." I pause. "I think we'll be looking over our shoulders for the rest of our lives. Being with me makes you a target until the day you die." I say.

"I don't understand, I'm giving you the knife back. Why would I still be a target?" he asks.

"The demons would use you to force me to give them the knife if they found out I had it. I couldn't live with myself, knowing you would be sacrificed. I wouldn't be able to give up the knife no matter what. I hope you understand." I say.

"In some crazy way, I guess I do understand." He says. "What are the chances of the demons finding out you have the knife?"

Victoria knew something and so did the demon that killed Elle. This means others are figuring out Pine Hill is a likely place to look. I can't take any chances with your life." I say.

"What if I'm willing to be a sacrifice?" He asks.

"I already told you. I can't let that happen." I say and move close to him.

"But, what if?" Ash challenges me again.

I press my forehead against Ash's. "No, I won't let that be an option."

"Okay." Ash says and I smile a fake smile. I push him back when he leans forward. His eyes follow me when I climb out of my bed and move across the cool floor. "Seriously," Ash says stretching over my bed on his back. I smile as he looks up at me. "What do you want to do today?"

I shrug. "What do you want to do?" I ask him. He sits upright and looks past me. I turn to see what he is looking at.

"Something outside," he tells me after I've turned around.

I'm not sure why he would want to go outside, it's freezing and where would we go? The woods? I don't think so! "No thanks, I think that it's too cold outside."

Ash frowns. "Well there's nothing to do inside either." He argues. He is right, there is nothing to do.

"Maybe we could just talk." I suggest. Ash's face turns red. "What?" I ask him.

"Nothing." He says quickly.

I roll my eyes. "Alright Ash."

Ash follows me out of the bedroom. I stop and stare at the bow sitting there next to the wall. I reach down, pick it up and stare at it. Ash senses my uneasiness and starts to take the bow from me. I grip it, and he lets go. Out of nowhere, I think back to my birthday and how delightful Elle was. I think about how she looked when she was dying. Her brown hair tangled, her chocolate color eyes empty, her tiny body curled up next to me. I try to erase that image out of my mind. I want to remember her as my beautiful and playful sister. "I miss her." I say and look at Liam.

Ash just stares at me. "What?" he asks.

"I think I need sometime by myself today." I say and put the bow back. Ash moves close to me and I step away from him.

"So I can't kiss you goodbye?" he asks.

"I'm not sure about anything anymore, I miss my sister and I need sometime alone to think." I look at him hoping he can understand this. He gently reaches out and brushes his hand against mine. I don't respond.

"I'll give you time to be alone with your thoughts." I think he realizes he can't help me this time. "Please don't make any life altering decisions while I'm away."

I gaze at the ground. "I promise. I just have a lot to think about. My future without Elle and my future with," I stop mid-sentence. "Thanks for giving me some space," I whisper.

Ash pulls my chin up so that I face him. "You may

not know at this moment who you'll spend your future with, but I have a feeling you'll choose Liam."

I back away from him. "I don't even know the answer to my future." We both go silent. "I do know that I need the knife back so nothing bad will happen to you. I'll stop by your house later to get it." I start walking him to the door.

He whirls around and kisses me. Not like the kisses he normally gives me or even something that Liam would do. It's entirely different, and I can't explain it.

He pulls away quickly and walks out the door. I gently shut the door and lean my back against the cold wood thinking about that kiss.

The day is dragging by slowly after Ash left me alone. I think of Elle and weep some. I think of Liam and Ash and cry some more. I wander through the house picking up some of the mess and even move furniture around to kill time and to think. I make something to eat and take a long time to eat it. I'm not hungry, I'm just wasting time. I grab a book off the shelf and randomly open it to page 84. I read the words, but I don't know what the story is about. I don't remember the last time I had this much time to myself. I start to realize that I need to be with Ash. I look up and see it's four o'clock. I grab my coat and head to Ash's house to get the knife and tell him I want him to be my future.

On my way to Ash's house, I run into Liam. "Hey, Liam." I say hoping he won't ask me if I made a decision.

"Where are you going?" he asks.

"I'm on my way to Ash's house to get the knife." I say

"I'll come with you." He says.

"I'd rather you not, but thanks for offering to walk with me." I try to keep my answers concise.

He grabs my arm and makes me face him. "You want to be with Ash." He pauses. "I can tell by the way you're acting." He says with hurt in his eyes.

"I can't lie to you Liam. We've been friends a long time and you're right. I'm choosing Ash to spend my life with. Please understand that we're friends and I love you as a friend, but my heart belongs to Ash." I say.

"See here's the problem. I don't understand Serena, but what can I do about it? I can't *make* you love me." Liam leaves me standing there and disappears into the distance.

I stand there trying to be strong about the decisions I've made. After a few minutes of waiting for Liam to return to try and convince me I'm making a mistake, I realize he's not coming back and continue on my way to Ash's house. I'm surprised Liam took the news as well as he did. Maybe he's tired of fighting for me and that's why he didn't come back to persuade me to into changing my mind.

I reach Ash's house and before I knock on the door, it swings open and there's Drew trying to hurry past me. I hear Ash in the background yelling. Ash runs to the door and stops when he sees me standing there.

"What's going on?" I ask.

"Drew took the knife and used it to cut up some fish he caught." Ash says out of breath.

He says out of breath.

"Okay, it's sharp enough to cut up fish." I say chuckling.

"That's not the problem. He left the knife down by

the river." He's pushing past me. "We are on our way to get it now." He sounds panicked.

"I'm coming with you." I say worried that the knife will be gone. On our way I think what if someone found the knife? What if a demon found it? "It's got to be there." I tell Ash as I pass him and catch up to Drew.

Drew's face is pink from running. "You didn't know, Drew." After that, there is no conversation between the three of us until we reach the lake. I look around. Dead cattails droop over the edge of the water that's glazed lightly with ice.

"Well," Ash speaks first. Drew and I turn to face him. "Where is it?" Drew rushes around the side of the small lake. Ash follows him, but I catch his arm.

"Take it easy on your brother Ash; at least he didn't lose it."

"Uh, guys!" Drew calls anxiously. Ash and I look at each other and then stare at Drew.

"That's not a good sign," mutters Ash as he takes off to meet his brother. I am close behind.

"I swear the knife was right here!" Drew says and points to a large cleared spot in the powdery snow. "It seemed to just have disappeared!"

Ash opens his mouth to yell at Drew, but he looks at me and slowly closes his mouth. Instead, he says calmly, "We have to find it." No one moves. "Anyone care to help me find it?" Drew drops to his knees and clears away more snow. I sink to my knees and swiftly sweep away the light snow. I look at Ash as he brushes away the snow. He's desperately trying to cover his frustration about the missing knife.

My hand connects with something cold and hard. I stop. "Ash! I think I found it!"

He gets up and runs over to me. I grip the knife and hold it up. Ash takes the knife from me and holds it in front of Drew. "I'm going to kill you with this!"

Even though Ash was joking, Drew runs away. Long awkward minutes pass before Ash and I look at each other. When we do, we both burst out laughing until we almost cry. While I try to catch my breath, Ash wraps his arms around me. Once I start to breathe normally again I look up at him.

"You could have been nicer to your *only* brother," I tell him.

He smiles. "I know, but I was so freaked out that something might happen to you I didn't really think of anything else at the moment." My eyes flit to the knife and back to Ash.

"I wish I could just forget," I whisper and gently leave his arms.

"Forget what?" Ash asks and frowns.

"That werewolves, demons, and powerful knives exist." I sit down with my head between my knees. Ash walks toward me and sits so close I feel his warm breath on my face.

"Serena," his voice is soft.

"Yeah," I say quietly; scared of saying something to make him move.

He puts his arm around my shoulder. "Those things exist and there is nothing either one of us can do to change it."

I raise my head to look at him. "How is it you still love me knowing what you know?" I ask.

Ash pulls away and smiles. "It doesn't matter if there are demons, werewolves, and…" he grins wider. "Liam." I smile with him. "They can't tear us apart unless we let them."

I want to believe him, but I have feelings for Liam that I don't understand. It is predestined that Liam and I belong together and I'm fighting it. I want to be with Ash. I close my eyes and feel his warm breath move across my face to my ear.

"I promise that I won't let anything come between us." I smile knowing that he tends to keep his promise.

"Isn't this precious?" A callous voice hisses from behind Ash and me. We whip around to see a creature hovering over us with rotting brown and gray colored skin, and fangs that gleam when the sunlight strikes them. "My source was right. He said you'd be here."

I stand up and step closer to it. "What are you talking about?" I yell.

It grins and scans me from head to toe as if he were assessing its competition.

It takes a step forward. "There's a rumor that you possess something I want." Its scaly wings expand and then collapse.

"I have no idea what you're talking about." I say with confidence. I'm glad we found the knife before the creature did.

"It doesn't matter, I'm not here for you," the demon circles around me and spreads its wings. It flaps it wings and circles over us and then lands next to Ash. Ash's face drains of all color. "I'm here for him."

My eyes dart around trying to find a large rock to throw at the demon. About two feet away, I see a rock sticking out of the snow. I pray it's not solidified to the cold ground. I use both hands to loosen it from the ground. The rock won't budge and so I go to plan B and shed my human form.

I jump protectively in front of Ash and snarl. "Your kind killed my only sister, Elle. You won't take another person from me again."

The demon grips my shoulder and sinks his claws into my flesh. I whimper. "You don't have a choice in the matter."

I lunge at the demon. It flies out of reach from me and swoops down. I try to grab it, but miss. I stay close to Ash and wait for the demon to make its next move. It lands behind Ash and starts to lunge for the knife that Ash is holding in his hands. I leap at the demon and sink my teeth into its side. The taste of its flesh is vile. It stumbles back. This demon wasn't as large as the others I've seen. The demon is mumbling something in another language. I can't understand what it's saying. I only hope it's not calling for backup.

I don't allow it time to make the next move. I lunge for the demon's neck and rip flesh. Just before I toss the flesh from my mouth, the demon says Liam's name.

"What did you say?" I ask.

The demon stares at me and said, "Liam said your friend has the Dagger of Death. Give it to me and I won't destroy him."

I watch as the demon is grasping its open wound. I can't believe Liam would do that to me. "It seems you were wrong. I do have a choice in the matter." With that, I leaped at the demon's throat and ripped out another chunk of flesh. This time, the demon slumped back and died. I stood there watching it to make sure it was dead before turning back into my human form. After a few minutes the demon's body turned to ash and blew away with the wind.

I look back to see Ash standing there grasping the knife. I change back to my human form and run to him. He stands there stiff as I try to pry the knife from his hands. He doesn't move and I wonder if he's in shock. "Ash, let go of the knife." I plead.

Finally, he stares at me for a second and then at the knife. He slowly loosens his grip and I take the knife. "Are you ok?" I ask. He doesn't answer me. "Ash, answer me!" I shake him.

"Liam." He says quietly.

I start thinking about what the demon said and realized Ash must have heard it also. "The demon was lying. Liam would never tell a demon you had the knife. That would be risking our kind if the demon took possession of the Dagger of Death." I try to convince Ash, but deep down, I knew Liam did sell us out.

Ash looks at me, with rage in his eyes. "Liam knew you would protect the knife at all cost. He was counting on you saving the knife and not me." He reaches out and takes the knife from me.

"I think we need to talk to Liam before we start making accusations." I say.

"I think you're trying to defend the guy. What changed to make him want to do this?"

"You may be right Ash. On my way to your house, I run into Liam. I told him that I wanted to be with you forever. I was surprised at how well he took the news." I think about what that short conversation with Liam may have cost me. "Give me the knife Ash."

Ash stands there with a blank stare. I try to change the subject.

"Hey, you know that kiss you gave me earlier today made my head spin. I don't know why, but I liked the feeling."

"You chose me?" He asks.

"Yes."

"How do I know you won't change your mind?" He moves closer and takes my hand.

"I love you Ash. I want us to be together forever and I hope you still want that also." I feel a tear coming down my cheek.

"I love you too Serena. I've always loved you, fangs and all." He jokes around and shows his beautiful straight teeth.

"I will love you…forever and ever." The sound of my voice rings in my head like an echo. He leans forward to kiss me.

Here it comes again, I think, and my head starts spinning again. I close my eyes in anticipation of his lips touching mine. I wait and when he doesn't touch me, I open my eyes and study his messy hair, and his brown eyes looking into mine. I close my eyes again, waiting for his kiss.

I smile, and Ash's lips kiss my chin and he pulls back. "What?" He laughs a bit when he hears me chuckling.

"Nothing, I want to know what you're doing," I say and open my eyes. His are already open; his big, brown eyes are shining.

"You want to know that I'm kissing you?" he asks and studies my face.

I smile, and my eyes trail the snow covered ground. I sit down and swirl my finger in the snow. "No, how you're making me so … dizzy, drunk with your touch. How do you do it?"

His face twists into confusion. "What are you talking about?" he insists.

"It's almost like that sleep syrup I had, but it only affects my head. How do you do it?" I ask again.

His eyebrows rise and he smirks. "Have you ever been dizzy before when I kissed you?"

My face goes red. "Yes, but not this much." I can tell he's making mental notes and continues.

"Then it must be the moment. You're so caught up in it and—"

"That's it! Thanks, I thought I was crazy," I say just to shut him up.

He takes my hand in his and twists it around. The ring glows, and he seems satisfied. "This ring looks perfect on your finger. I hope it will deter other guys from flirting with you," he says and sets my hand down.

"Sorry to break it to you, but the ring isn't magical. They flirt with me all of the time. I have to beat them off me every day." I laugh.

I press my forehead to his and just stay that way until I remember that the wedding is in a few days. I stand up.

"I need to go to the market and pickup some stuff for the wedding. Do you want to go with me?" I ask and pat him on the back.

Ash is in deep thought and doesn't respond. "Hey, did you hear what I just said?" I ask softly.

Ash looks up and smiles. "I'd love to go with you, but I owe my best man an apology and I want to tell him the wedding is back on. You go ahead and I'll meet up with you tomorrow at your house." He smiles and kisses me on the cheek.

"Okay. I'll go to the market in the morning. It's getting late. I'll see you in the afternoon." I walk home and for the first time, things are going my way.

As I arrive at home, I stop and stare at the house. I start to remember my parents playing with me and Elle outside. They chased us around the yard until we were exhausted. I remember my dad taking me out to the woods behind the house and teaching me to shoot small game animals with the bow. I picture my mom cooking dinner for us and my dad sneaking a spoonful of whatever my mother was making. She knew he was doing it and would fuss at him.

I wonder if that's how Ash and I will be. I go inside the house and cook soup out of the little bit of food that was in the cupboards. I start to clean up when I hear a knock on the door.

I open the door to find Aunt Lila standing there with a bag of groceries and some other bags at her feet.

"Hello Serena, would you mind helping me with these bags?" She says as she enters the house. I reach down and grab the bags and shut the door.

I follow her to the kitchen and she set the bag on the table and begins to unpack it. "I haven't seen you around lately." She says concerned.

"I've been really busy these days." I say.

"How are you doing with Elle gone?" she asks and doesn't look at me. She continues to pull items from the bags and puts them in the cupboard.

"It's been difficult for me to adjust my life without her. I think about her all the time." I say.

"Sorry I haven't been around much. I haven't been well lately and I'm not getting out much." She says.

"Nothing serious I hope. Have you seen the doctor?" I ask.

"No, I think its old age and a doctor can't fix that." She says with a laugh.

"I almost forgot to tell you. I'm getting married and I'd like you to come." I smile not sure how she will react to the news.

She drops a can of beans on the floor and it shatters. "I'll get a broom and clean that up." I say and rush off to the other room and come back with the broom and clean up the mess.

"You're getting married? When did this happen?" She asks.

"I sense you're not happy about this." I frown.

"No, it just took me by surprise. You just lost Elle and I'm not sure you're old enough to get married. Is it because you're…"

I interrupt her, "No!" I yell. "I'm in love with Ash and we are getting married."

"You're too young Serena. Your parents wouldn't approve of it." She says.

"My parents haven't been around in a long time and I'm sure they won't interfere with my life now." I say knowing she doesn't know that they are dead.

"Why is it so important to get married now?" she asks.

"It's my life and I want to be with Ash forever." I say.

"Forever is a long time for some people. Is he a werewolf?" She asks.

This takes me by surprise because we never discussed this subject. I guess I've always known that she knows about the werewolves since her sister is one. It's kind of hard to hide it. "He's a human." I say quietly.

"Does he know you're a werewolf?" she asks.

"Yes, he knows what I am and he still wants to marry me." I say.

"That forever I mentioned is not going to happen for him. Are you ready for that?" she asks.

"I never thought about it like that. I love him and that's what matters." I declare.

"It's your life Serena. Though it's not been an easy one so far, I don't see the harm in you finding your way through this life with a little bit of happiness. You never mentioned the boy's name."

"Ash. His name is Ash Parker." I say.

"When is the big day?" she asks.

"The wedding is Saturday at noon. It's not a legal ceremony, but it would mean a lot to have you there." I plead.

"If I'm feeling well, I will be there." She forces a smile. "It's getting late. I need to be going." She reached in her pocket and pulls out some money. "You'll need this." She says.

I take the money and go to hug her but she backs away. I feel awkward, so I just say thank you.

Aunt Lila leaves and I go to my room and lay across the bed thinking about what I need to do tomorrow. Before long my eyes close and I fall asleep.

I awake to the sunlight beaming through the white curtains. I pull the covers over my head and try to fall back asleep. No such luck. I'm wide awake thinking about everything I need to do today.

I jump out of bed and throw on some clothes. I tidy

up the house and finish off the soup I made yesterday. I boil some water and fill the tub so I can wash up. The water doesn't stay warm long forcing me to take a quick bath. I find myself forgetting all the bad that has happened as I'm getting ready to go out the door.

First stop the market to buy some flowers and some food for the wedding. Then I need to stop by the church to see if the minister will agree to marry us unofficially. The sun has melted most of the snow and the temperature feels warmer. I grab a light jacket and head to town. My mood is light and I'm smiling thinking about the wedding and how wonderful it will be to have Ash as a husband. Wow. That sounded weird. I say Serena Parker out loud. I keep repeating Mrs. Serena Parker over and over. It has a nice ring to it.

I change my mind and decide to speak to the minister before buying the flowers and food. I run up the large steps and open the enormous doors to the Church. I haven't been to Church since my parents left us. It feels familiar, but awkward. No one is in the Church and I call out to see if anyone is there. My voice echoes across the room. Finally, I see an old man in a robe open a door from the back of the room. He smiles and walks towards me. I meet him half way and hold out my hand to shake his. He shakes my hand and holds the shake with his other hand.

"Serena, it's been a long time since you were here. I'm so sorry about what happened to Elle. What brings you to Church today?" his voice is kind and gentle.

"I'm sorry it's been a long time, but I have a big favor to ask you." I look around the empty Church to make sure no one is listening. "I'm getting married on Saturday and I was hoping you could perform the ceremony." I say quietly so my voice doesn't echo.

"I think you're a little young to get married." He smiles.

"Yes, you're right. I'm too young to get married legally, but I want to get married in a spiritual setting. That's what matters most to me at this time. Don't you agree?" I ask.

"Well the law is the law and if I were to agree to marry you, the law wouldn't recognize it as a legal marriage." He says.

"Right, I understand, but I'm not concerned with the law. I can pay you a small fee for performing the ceremony," as I reach in my pocket and pull out the money Aunt Lila gave me.

"Put your money away Serena. Are your plans to marry in the Church?"

"No sir, we want to be married by a river not far from here. Is that a problem?" I ask.

"No it's not a problem. I'm happy that you've found love with…what is the young man's name?" he asks.

"Ash Parker."

"I know his parents. Ash doesn't come to Church with his parents anymore. If I remember right, he's a good boy." He looks up to the right as if he were trying to recall something.

"Yes, he is a good man," I correct him.

"What time is the wedding?" he asks.

"One o'clock" I say with a smile. "I will draw a map of how to get there and bring it back to you this afternoon."

"I can do this for you if you promise to come back to Church and bring your new husband with you." He smiles back and puts his hand on my shoulder.

"I think we can do that sir. Thank you for agreeing to marry us." I smile back at him and he walks back to the room he came from.

I walk out of the Church and the sunlight blinds me at first. In my mind I start running down the list of things I will need for the wedding and head to the market. Since there won't be that many people at the wedding, I settle on buying cheese, bread, juice, and other snacks that I can easily throw together. I decide I can hunt whatever meat I'll have at the wedding.

I see a couple of girls from school pass by I look the other way knowing as soon as I do they begin to whisper. I turn my head back around, sure enough, one is whispering to the other.

I make my way to the little flower shop that smells of dead lilacs and other blooming flowers. I see bunches of fresh flowers and make my way over to see if there are any lilacs and white roses. Elle's favorite flowers were lilacs and white roses. As I look through the selection, I see yellow, white and red roses mixed together with greenery but I don't see any lilacs. I ask the lady behind the counter if she had any lilacs, but she said they weren't in season. Even though roses aren't in season either, they are popular so their seeds are planted inside the shop. I decide on the roses and ask if I could buy only the white roses. She nods and reaches in a bucket and pulled out a bunch of the flowers.

"How many would you like?" she asks.

"I'll take 24 white roses." I force a friendly smile; I'm not used to talking to strangers that don't want to kill me.

She starts to move but looks confused and turns back

to me. "Do you want all 24 bunched together or do you want me to divide them into two bunches?" Her thin black eyebrows rise.

I lean my elbows against the counter. "One bunch please."

She counts out 24 white roses and gently wraps them in a greenish clear plastic paper. "You can take these to the counter with your other items and pay for it there." She looks behind me and asks the lady standing there if she could help her. I have one last item to buy.

I head to the bakery and look at all the cakes behind the counter. An older man with dark grey eyes sees me standing there and asks if he can help me. "I'd like to buy a cake with white frosting," I tell him pointing to one of the cakes in the display case.

"What kind of batter would you like inside?" he asks.

"It doesn't matter." I say. "Can you decorate the top of the cake with white roses?" I ask.

"Yes, is this for a birthday?"

"No, it's for my wedding." I say.

The man starts laughing and grabs the cake from the display case and begins decorating it with white roses. I stand there for a minute and wonder if he thought I was joking. I didn't care. After a few minutes he shows me the cake. It was the most beautiful cake I've ever seen. He did a wonderful job adding the roses to the around the edges and three delicately placed in the middle. It looked like a garden of flowers.

I thanked him and took the cake, flowers and food to the lady the florist pointed me to. The temperature outside is nearly fifty degrees. The sun makes it feel warmer. I start to make my way across town, when I hear someone call my name. I turn to see it's Drew.

He runs over to me and I smile at him. "Can I help you with those groceries?" He asks.

"Thanks. Do you have time to help me carry them back to my house?" I ask.

He smiles. "Sure. I don't have anything going today." He grabs the bag with the flowers sticking out.

As we walk he starts talking about a girl he has a crush on in school. "I asked her out, but she said no. Can you believe she turned this handsome man down?" He points to his body and laughs. I laugh with him.

"Drew, I love you to pieces but you're barely a man. Anyway, she doesn't realize what she's missing." We laugh some more. We are almost to my house when Drew asks about the flowers.

"Are these white roses for Elle?" He asks.

"Sort of." I say.

"What do you mean?" He asks confused.

"Actually they are for the wedding on Saturday." I say looking at how beautiful the blooms are.

"What wedding?" he asks.

We reach my house and I set the bag down to open the door and look at Drew to see if he's joking. "Mine and Ash's wedding."

"I don't know whether to congratulate you or feel sorry for you." He laughs out loud and then says, "I wonder why Ash didn't say anything about it." He says.

"What do you mean he didn't say anything? He was going to tell you about it last night. He was going to ask you to be his best man." I say confused.

"I haven't seen Ash since he threatened to kill me

when I borrowed his precious knife." He says making a hand gesture like he's slitting his throat with his index finger.

"That doesn't make any sense. He said he was going home to tell you about it." I start to get a knot in my stomach. "Drew, take these groceries inside please. I have to find Ash," and I take off in the direction of Liam's house.

I take a shortcut through the woods. I run as fast as I can and jump over fallen branches on the path to Liam's house. It feels like I'm running in slow motion. I have a feeling Ash is confronting Liam about what the demon said. I pray I'm wrong. The thought of another close friend dying is making me sick to my stomach. I can't stop thinking that this is going to end bad for one of them. I reach the edge of the woods and see Liam's house in the distance. My eyes are drawn to the set of pine trees lining the edge of Liam's property. I see two figures struggling. As I run towards the pine trees, I see Liam in wolf form snap his large jaws at Ash. I stop dead in my tracks.

Liam backs up and growls. Liam leaps at Ash. My eyes widen and I scream Ash's name. He doesn't look towards me. I see Ash holding a shining object above his head. It's not Ash that I worry about now. I manage to push myself faster to stop Ash. "Ash, stop!" I cry out only to be muted by the pained yelps of Liam.

Ash jerks his head in my direction and drops the knife to his side. His jaw drops and he looks back to Liam who is lying on the ground pawing at the slice on the bottom of his chest. Liam transforms back into his human self.

I run past Ash and drop to my knees next to Liam. I

cover my mouth with my hand in shock and look back at Ash. Ash continues to stand above me and Liam. I lift his head above the ground and set it on my lap. "Liam, Liam I'm here now." I gently shake his arm.

"Serena," he moans and takes his hand away from his chest. A large tear in his flesh bleeds heavily.

I brush a strand of his black hair out of his eyes. "Does it hurt?" I ask, not sure if when you're a dying werewolf you can feel that much pain.

Liam shifts his head to the side. "No."

"Really?" I ask.

He looks at me. "No! It hurts a lot!" he says smiling. I smile back. I turn him flat on his back again.

"How can you joke around, Liam. This wound looks serious." I tell him.

"Serena, I know I've probably told you this a million times before, and I'm guessing most of those times you didn't listen to me, but I love you. Still. Until I take my last breath, I'm guessing that will be in a few minutes here."

I lean down and kiss his cheek. Despite Ash standing right by me, I tell Liam what I know he would want to hear. "I Love you too, Liam."

"You can't love someone who sent a demon after you!" Ash chimes in.

I hold a hand up for Ash to stop, without making eye contact. "Ash, please stop."

Liam attempts to raise his head, but sets it back down on my lap. "I didn't send a demon after anyone," Liam reaches for my hand. "Why would I do that to someone I love?"

I see Ash out of the corner of my eye turn toward

me. "Serena, he told me he sent the demon after me so I would be gone from your..." he pauses.

I tilt my head down closer to Liam. "Ash, this isn't the time."

Liam closes his eyes.

"Liam? Liam!" I shake him.

"What?" He coughs. I force a smile despite my desperate wanting to cry.

His eyes flicker from Ash, to me. He sucks in a deep breath. "Ash is lying."

Ash grits his teeth. "Don't you-"

"I love you, I always have. Not just because of the werewolf tradition. I honestly and truly wanted us to be together."

"You could have been the one, but now I will never know." I would have said more, but Ash grabs my arm at that moment and pulls me slightly back from Liam. Liam's head falls on to the ground.

"What are you saying?" he asks.

Without making eye contact, I break free from his grasp. "Why did you stab Liam?" I move back to Liam. Liam is slightly smiling. I lean close to his face. "Love you," I tell him and kiss his cheek. I hear footsteps and know that Ash is walking away.

"I can't stay here and listen to you confess your love to this monster." Ash yells to me. Liam's grin ends and he glances at Ash.

I run my fingers through his hair. "It's okay Liam. I'll stay here." When he doesn't move or respond, I lightly push on his arm. "Liam?" I can't hold the tears back any longer. "Liam!" Even though I know he's gone, I still try and make him respond.

As the sun begins to set, I stop shaking him and begging him to wake up, I sob quietly next to him. I look up to the sky. "Liam. I can't believe you're gone." I rest my head over his lifeless chest. No heart beat, no movement. I feel empty inside and cry some more.

"Told you so," Liam's voice rings out. Through the sky burning with bold oranges and blazing reds over a vivid sun.

I stand up and close my eyes trying to keep his image alive and inside me. I think back to the day he told me the story about the werewolves. I remember every word so clearly. I remember our last kiss and touched my lips and smiled. I gently place my hand over my neck and quietly whisper in his ear, "I'll miss you."

CHAPTER 14

A month later...

Aunt Lila stopped by the day of the wedding. I was surprised to see her and she was surprised to learn the wedding was cancelled. She didn't ask what happened and left me to sulk.

I have been avoiding Ash ever since Liam's death. I have nothing to say to him. Ash stopped by several times, but I wouldn't answer the door. He finally gave up after a few weeks and hasn't stopped by.

The flowers wilted and the food spoiled that I bought for the wedding ceremony. For some reason, I couldn't throw them out until today. Being away from Ash has made me think about my future without him.

I open the door and inhale a deep breath of crisp spring air. The temperature is warmer and the sun is shining. I stand outside my house enjoying the change of seasons. There are buds on the trees and the grass is trying to turn green. At a leisurely pace with a basket in one hand and money in my pocket, I head to the market.

"Two white roses please." I say to the lady who gave me the flowers for my wedding that never happened. She hands me the roses and I give her the money.

"Thanks cupcake. Next!" she yells. I move out of line and a little boy with black hair steps up. I don't leave. I watch the boy. There is something about his bright green eyes that are familiar. I shrug off the feeling and continue out the wooden door.

A strong breeze blows my hair in my face. I glance over at my roses and notice one of them is missing. I look around for it and see it fell out of the bag not far from my feet. I lean down to pick it up, extending my hand to grab it. My hand comes in contact with another and I pull back. I look up into brown eyes.

"Serena."

This is the first time I have looked in his eyes in over a month. My throat tightens. That familiar feeling of being in love starts to creep into my heart. All I want to do is run into his arms and kiss him. It takes me a couple of seconds to find the right words, but all I could say is, "Ash."